MYTHS & LEGENDS

Vic Parker

Miles
Kelly

CREATION MYTHOLOGY
10–63

GODS AND SPIRITS
64–123

EPIC HEROES AND ADVENTURES 124–199

MAGIC AND MYSTERY
200–255

LIFE AND LOVE
256–305

DESTRUCTION AND DEATH 306–369

Scandinavian stories

- **Norse mythology** comes from the Scandinavian people of the Bronze Age. They were the ancestors of the Vikings.

- **In the beginning** there was a huge emptiness called Ginnungagap. First, a fiery southern land called Muspelheim came into existence, then came a freezing northern land called Niflheim.

- **The fires eventually began to melt** the ice, and the dripping waters formed into the first being – a wicked Frost Giant named Ymir. More Frost Giants formed from Ymir's sweat.

- **The next being that grew** from the thawed ice was a cow called Audhumla. Audhumla licked an ice block into a male being called Buri.

- **Buri's grandchildren** were the first three Norse gods – Odin, Vili and Ve. They killed Ymir and threw his body into Ginnungagap.

- **Ymir's flesh, blood, bones**, hair, skull and brains became the earth, seas, mountains, forests, sky and clouds.

- **Dwarves came into existence** before human beings. They grew from maggots in Ymir's flesh.

- **Odin, Vili and Ve** created the first man, Ask, from an ash tree and the first woman, Embla, from an elm tree. The gods gave the humans a world called Midgard.

- **The gods tried** to keep the evil giants away from the humans and gods by giving them a separate land, Jotunheim.

- **The home of the gods was called** Asgard. It was connected to the world of humans by a rainbow bridge. The god Heimdall was set as watchman to make sure only gods and goddesses could cross it.

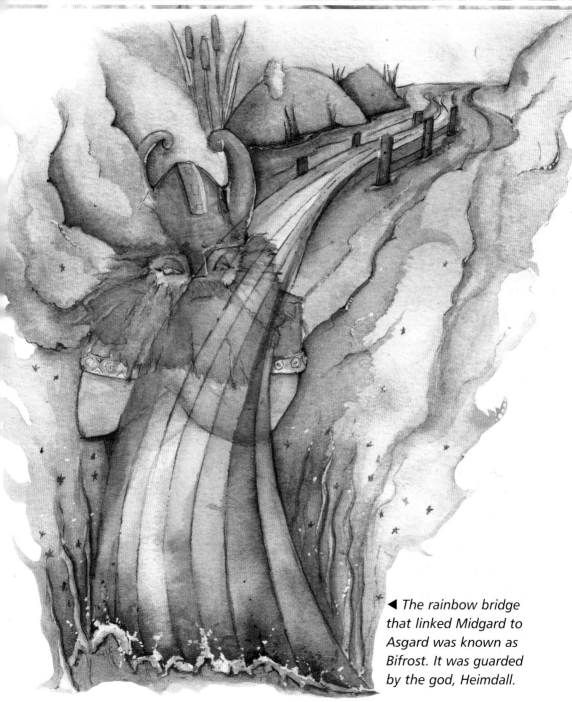

◀ The rainbow bridge that linked Midgard to Asgard was known as Bifrost. It was guarded by the god, Heimdall.

Ancient Greeks

■ **The earliest ancient Greeks**, Bronze Age farmers, worshipped the mother earth goddess, Gaea.

■ **Myths say that Gaea emerged** out of an emptiness called Chaos.

■ **Gaea gave birth** to the god of the mountains Ourea, the god of the sea Pontus, and the god of the sky Uranus.

■ **The next rulers** were the children of Gaea and Uranus – 12 immortals called the Titans.

■ **The children of the Titans**, Oceanus and Tethys, lived as spirits called nymphs in all the springs, rivers and seas of the world.

■ **The Titans**, Cronus and Rhea, had children who overthrew them. They became the next immortal rulers – the Greek gods and goddesses.

■ **Three Greek gods** divided the universe between them – Zeus ruled the earth, Poseidon ruled the seas, and Hades ruled the kingdom of the dead.

■ **Some myths** say that the most intelligent Titan, Prometheus, created the first man out of clay and water.

▶ *The Greeks built impressive temples to honour gods and goddesses. At 12 m in height, the magnificent statue of the Greek god Zeus at Olympia was constructed out of ivory and gold.*

▶ *In early Greek artworks, the Sphinx is a monster with a man's head, a lion's body and wings. Later artworks show the Sphinx with a woman's head and chest.*

■ **Other myths say that the chief god**, Zeus, created five races of human beings. The Gold Race lived in harmony with the gods and died peacefully. The Silver Race was quarrelsome and disrespectful, so Zeus wiped it out. The Bronze Race loved weapons and war, so brought death upon themselves. The Race of Heroes was so noble that Zeus took them to live on the islands of the blessed.

■ **Human beings of today** make up the Race of Iron. Myths predict that as no respect is shown for the earth, Zeus will eventually destroy it – and the human race.

Mesopotamia

■ **The oldest recorded mythology** in the world is from the Middle East, dating from 2500 BC.

■ **The Babylonian creation myth** grew from the Sumerian creation myth. It is called the Enuma Elish.

■ **The Enuma Elish** was found by archaeologists excavating Nineveh, Assyria in AD 1845. It was written on seven clay tablets in a language called cuneiform.

■ **According to this creation epic,** in the beginning the universe was made of salt waters (Mother Tiamat), sweet waters, (Father Apsu), and a mist (their son Mummu).

■ **The waters gave birth** to rebellious gods who overthrew Apsu and Mummu.

■ **Tiamat and her followers**, led by the god Kingu, were conquered by the Babylonian god, Marduk, in a battle of powerful magic.

■ **Marduk had four eyes** and four ears, so he could see and hear everything. Fire spurted from his mouth and haloes blazed from his head.

■ **As the new ruler,** Marduk made Tiamat's body into the earth and sky, and appointed gods to rule the heavens, the earth and the air in between.

■ **Human beings** were created out of the god Kingu's blood. Marduk made them build a temple at Babylon to honour himself and the other gods.

■ **Every spring**, Babylon was in danger of devastating flooding from the mighty rivers Tigris and Euphrates. Historians believe that the Enuma Elish may have been acted as a pantomime to please Marduk, so he kept order and prevented the flooding.

▼ *The Sumerians of Mesopotamia built large stepped temples of mud-bricks called ziggurats to worship their gods and goddesses.*

Aboriginal beliefs

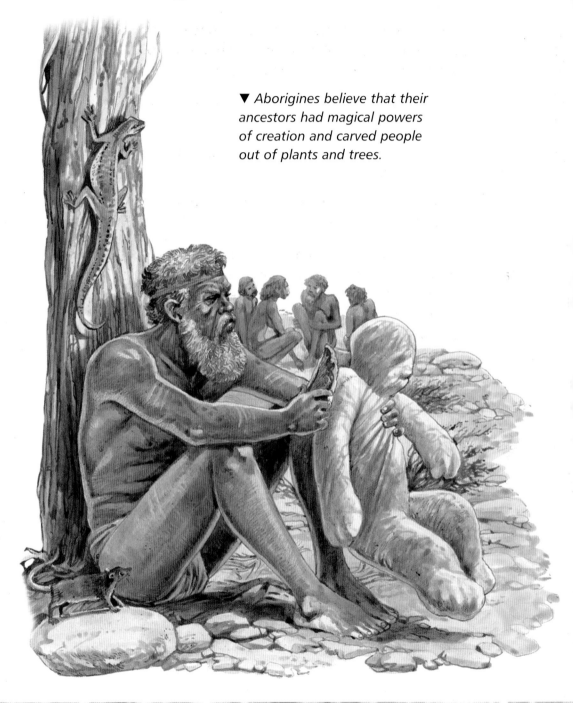

▼ Aborigines believe that their ancestors had magical powers of creation and carved people out of plants and trees.

- **The mythology of Australia** comes from wandering tribes of people collectively called Aborigines. Historians believe that they are descended from survivors of the Stone Age.

- **The creation mythology** of the Aborigines is called the Dreamtime.

- **There are various Dreamtime stories**, all originating from different tribal groups.

- **Most Dreamtime mythology** says that in the beginning, the earth was just a dark plain.

- **According to Aboriginal beliefs from central Australia**, their ancestors slept beneath the earth, with the sun, the moon and the stars. Eventually the ancestors woke up and wandered about the earth in the shapes of humans, animals and plants, shaping the landscape.

- **Central Australian myths say that people** were carved out of animals and plants by their ancestors, who then went back to sleep in rocks, trees or underground – where they are to this day.

- **Aborigines from south eastern Australia** believed that heroes from the sky shaped the world and created people.

- **Tribes from the northeast** believed that everything was created by two female ancestors who came across the sea from the land of the dead.

- **A wise rainbow snake** plays an important part in many Dreamtime myths. She forms the valleys and mountains by slithering through the featureless land.

- **Aborigines believe** that even the harshest landscape is sacred because the life of the ancestors runs through it.

The Beginning of Life

An Aboriginal myth

L ong, long ago was the
Dreamtime. Everywhere was
bare, flat and empty. There
was only stillness and quietness
all over the surface of the world.

However, underneath the
surface, deep in the earth's crust,
all sorts of creatures were sleeping.
Animals, birds and reptiles lay cocooned
in the land, dreaming peacefully.

One day the Rainbow Serpent opened her eyes and found

herself in complete darkness. Flexing and stretching her coils, she began to push her way through the earth. Finally, she broke through the surface, bursting out into the sunlight. The featureless land stretched in all directions. She set off to explore.

Slithering all over the land, the Rainbow Serpent's strong winding body carved out valleys and heaped up land into ridges. She journeyed for many moons, travelling over the whole earth until she arrived back where she had started. Exhausted, she coiled herself up and rested.

After a long nap, it occured to her that all the other creatures were still asleep deep inside the earth. With as much energy as she could summon, the Rainbow Serpent called and called, and gradually, her voice penetrated the layers of the earth and began to stir the creatures from their deep slumbers.

The frogs awoke first. Slowly, they began to move up through the earth, with their bodies full of water. Delighted, the Rainbow Serpent tickled the frogs, making them laugh so hard that they coughed up their stores of water, which flowed out over the earth. Some of the water gushed into channels and pits formed by the Rainbow Serpent's wanderings, creating streams, rivers, waterfalls and lakes. Other trickles of water ran away over the soil and were absorbed by the land. In these places, tiny green shoots appeared. Soon, in all directions there were patches of soft grass, clumps of leafy bushes and bright flowers, and clusters of tall, spreading trees.

As the land sprang to life, all the other reptiles, birds and animals burst out from under the ground. The Rainbow Serpent led them across the earth and they all found suitable homes. The birds were delighted to swoop through the skies and nest in the treetops. The reptiles were comfortable sheltering among cool stones and damp, shady nooks and crannies. The Rainbow Serpent was acknowledged by all as the mother of life. She set laws, so that all the creatures could thrive together and the earth remain healthy forever.

As time passed, the Rainbow Serpent noticed that some creatures were particularly excellent at keeping her laws. She gave these creatures human form and told them that they were in charge of looking after the land and everything that lived in it. Each human had a totem pole of the tribe they came from, whether from an animal, reptile or bird. The Rainbow Serpent instructed all the tribes that they were allowed to eat creatures from any totem pole except their own – that way, there would be enough food for everyone.

The Rainbow Serpent chose other creatures that she was very pleased with and turned them into rock. They were sent to stand forever as hills and mountains, acting as the guardians of the tribes living on the land.

And so the tribes and the land lived and prospered together. A man called Biami grew to be an exceptionally wise human. Knowledgeable, honest and kind, he took great care of the earth.

When he became old, the Rainbow Serpent did not let him die, but gave him a spirit form, so he could live forever among the tribes as a protector.

It wasn't long before Biami was faced with evil. Calmly, Biami cast the man and his selfish, devious ways out from his tribe. Abandoned and angry, the wicked man used all his cunning to discover how to take on spirit form. He became an evil spirit called the Bunyip.

Alarmed, Biami warned the tribes to keep away from the Bunyip and have nothing to do with him. Even more furious, the Bunyip determined to have revenge. He decided to use his evil to wreak chaos among the tribes and bring as much trouble and sorrow to everyone as he could. The Bunyip raged and swore hatred, and threatened to steal any tribe member he could lay his hands on – and devour them.

From that day to this, everyone has lived in fear of the Bunyip. He lurks in gloomy, remote places such as waterholes and rainforests, luring travellers to their deaths. He delights in snatching and eating children, and ensnaring people to become his evil slaves for eternity.

Ancient Egyptians

■ **The mythology of ancient Egypt** may go back as far as 4000 BC, when the land was populated by farming peoples.

■ **Each area of Egypt** originally worshipped different gods. Their stories spread and merged, so there are many versions, and some gods are known in different forms.

■ **According to Egyptian mythology,** in the beginning the universe was filled with dark waters.

■ **The first god was Ra**, the god of the sun and light. A blue lotus flower appeared on Nun, the waters of chaos, and unfurled its petals to reveal Ra, who then created the world and everything in it.

■ **The first gods**, Shu, the god of air, and Tefnut, the goddess of water were created from Ra's spittle.

■ **Humans were created** one day when Shu and Tefnut wandered into the dark wastes and got lost. Ra sent his eye to find them. When they were reunited, Ra's tears of joy turned into people.

▶ *The sun god, Ra, is often pictured holding an ankh. This is the sign of life and the key to the underworld.*

▶ *Hieroglyph means 'sacred carving'. Each picture stands for an object or an idea or a sound. The image of the scarab beetle is very important to Egyptian mythology, meaning 'to come into being'.*

■ **The world was created** when Shu and Tefnut gave birth to two children – Nut, the sky goddess, and Geb, the earth god.

■ **Ancient Egyptians believed** that Ra originally lived in the world with humans. When he grew old, humans tried to rebel against him, so he went to live in the sky.

■ **Ra was so angry** with the humans that he sent Sekhmet, the goddess of war, to destroy them, but was stopped by the other gods and goddesses.

■ **Myths were written down** in hieroglyphic writing. This system was invented around 3000 BC, when Upper Egypt and Lower Egypt united into one kingdom.

Native Americans

■ **Native American myths** come from the first people to live in North America. They spread there from Asia around 15,000 years ago when the two continents were linked by ice.

■ **Native Americans settled** in many different tribes. Although each tribe had its own myths and legends, they all shared many beliefs. The stories were passed down through generations by word of mouth.

■ **Many tribes believed** that everything in the world is part of one harmonious creation. Harming any part of it would upset the balance.

■ **In Iroquois myths,** mother earth fell into a lake from a land beyond the sky. The animals helped create the sun, the moon and the stars.

■ **According to the Algonquian,** Michabo the Great Hare created the earth, from a grain of sand from the bottom of the ocean.

■ **The Maidu tribe held the belief** that the gods Kodoyanpe and Coyote floated on the surface of a vast expanse of water and one day decided to create the world.

◀ *In Native American myth, the Thunderbird was a mighty eagle that represented the power of storms. The beating of its wings sounded like thunder, and lightning flashed from its eyes.*

▲ *The Iroquois tribe lived in an eastern area of North America now known as New York State. Native Americans wore eagle feathers, often in their headdresses, for various reasons. They can represent the strength of the eagle, or spiritual power.*

■ **Navajo mythology stated** that the first man and woman were created when four gods ordered the winds to blow life into two ears of corn.

■ **Many Native American myths** say that when the world was created, humans and animals lived together.

■ **Native Americans** believed that all creation is ruled over by a supreme spirit. Different tribes gave him different names, including Amotken.

■ **In 1855, Henry Wadsworth Longfellow** wrote an epic poem called *The Song of Hiawatha*, about a real Native American hero. Many aspects of his myth differ from reality. For instance, in the poem, Hiawatha is Iroquois, when in reality he was Algonquian.

Raven and the Source of Light

A Native American myth

*I*n the far north there is nothing but frozen snow and ice in all directions. The air is so cold, the people wear furs to keep warm. With the howling winds and biting frosts, every step is a labour of strength. This freezing, unwelcoming land is where the Inuit people call home.

Once, these freezing deserts lay in total darkness all year round. The Inuit found the dark even worse than the cold. In the darkness, they had to build igloos, fish at ice-holes, and hunt polar bears. Time was meaningless. It was simply impossible to tell whether it was morning or night – the darkness just went on endlessly.

As a way of escaping from the crushing blackness around them, the Inuit liked to spend time indoors, telling stories. Huddling around a small fire, their faces lit by the flames, they would dream. The best storyteller was the Inuit's friend, Raven. Raven had come from a faraway place – further than the Inuit could trek on their snowshoes. He told of sights and sounds that they had never seen or heard.

"Where I come from, it is bright during the day and only dark at night. The brightness is more brilliant than your fires and lamps. It lights up everything as far as the eye can see, and floods the world with fantastic colours. I have seen green grass, red rooftops, purple mountains, yellow beaches, blue seas, pink flowers, brown animals, and orange fish. The daylight brings heat, too. I have basked and bathed in warm breezes. I have felt the thrill of swooping down into chill shadows and then soaring out into blazing brightness that warms my wings."

The Inuit never tired of hearing Raven talk about daylight. How wonderful it sounded! But Raven's heart grew heavy with sadness that his friends could not see daylight for themselves. He began to wonder if there was a way that he could bring them some.

One day, Raven silently flew into the darkness, determined to find daylight and bring some back for the Inuit. Raven flew and flew … further and further and further … until his beak was frozen, his wings ached and his eyes grew tired of peering

into the darkness. He began to worry that he might drop with cold and exhaustion before making it to the daylight lands.

The Inuit were so good and kind. They became friends when he accidentally flew into their dark, frozen wastes and became lost. Instead of shooting him for food, the Inuit let him rest by their fires, sharing their fish and seal meat with him. Raven had never had companionship like this before. Now, it was his turn to do something for his friends. Spurred on, he kept flying … further and further and further … until finally, the darkness and cold began to fade. Gradually warmth surrounded him, and the colours of the earth flooded his vision. He had arrived in the daylight lands!

Raven circled around over the land, looking for where the daylight might come from. He picked out the largest, grandest house for miles around, and swooped down. Whoever owned the largest, grandest house must be the most important person. And surely the most important person would be in charge of the daylight.

Landing on the windowsill, Raven peered inside. He saw a little boy, and an old man, wrapped in richly coloured cloths decorated with beads, bones and feathers – he was clearly a great chief. When the chief wasn't looking, Raven flew inside.

"Ask your grandfather for a piece of daylight to play with," he whispered in the boy's ear. Then he shot up and hid among the rafters.

The little boy was delighted at the idea. "Grandfather! May I play with a piece of daylight?" he cried.

"Daylight is far too precious to be played with, my boy. Perhaps I can tell you a story about my great ancestors?" his grandfather offered. But his grandson didn't want to hear a story.

"I want a piece of daylight!" the child howled, beginning to cry.

The little boy sobbed and gulped and moaned, and wouldn't stop even though his grandfather hugged him and promised him all sorts of treats. At last the chief could stand it no longer. He reached up, snapped off a piece of daylight and tied it to a long string. As he handed the string to his beaming grandson, Raven swooped down and grabbed it in his beak! He sped out of the window, heading northwards across the skies.

Out of the darkness, the Inuit saw a strange glimmer appear above them. It spread and glowed brighter, making the snow and ice glitter all around. Suddenly they saw Raven, flying closer with a piece of daylight! By the time he arrived, their entire world was bright and light. Daylight was even more wonderful than they had imagined!

Ever since then, the piece of daylight has been enough to light the Inuit lands for half of every year. The Inuit only have to spend winter in darkness – and all thanks to their friend, Raven.

Who were the Celts?

▲ The Celts made tools, weapons, armour and jewellery from many different metals. Nobles wore gold and jewellery, decorated with intricate, flowing patterns. This heavy, twisted neckband is called a torque.

■ **After the Roman invasion** of Britain in the first century AD, the Celts were a people who lived mainly in Ireland, Scotland, Wales, Cornwall and northern France.

■ **Celtic myths were told** as stories by poets called bards, and priests called druids. Christian monks later wrote down the tales.

■ **In Celtic creation mythology**, Ireland existed at the beginning of time and covered the whole world.

■ **According to Celtic myth**, the first people to settle in Ireland all died in a great flood.

■ **The second race of settlers** were male and female gods called the Partholons. They fought off a race of invading monsters called the Fomorians, before being wiped out by a plague.

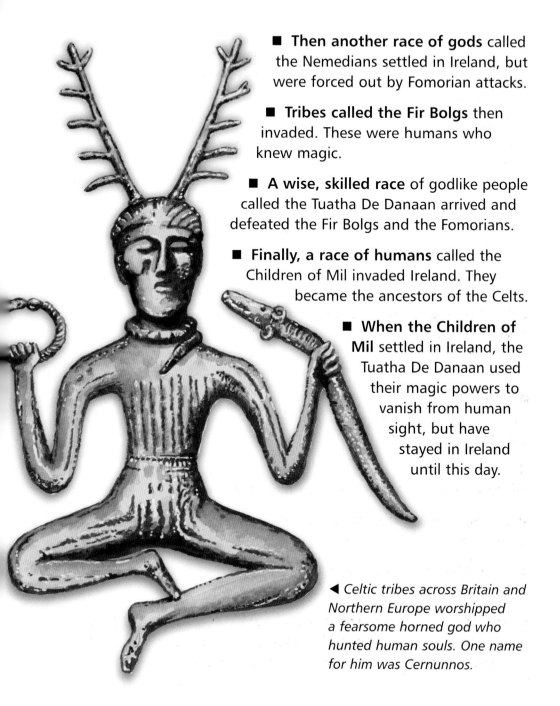

- **Then another race of gods** called the Nemedians settled in Ireland, but were forced out by Fomorian attacks.

- **Tribes called the Fir Bolgs** then invaded. These were humans who knew magic.

- **A wise, skilled race** of godlike people called the Tuatha De Danaan arrived and defeated the Fir Bolgs and the Fomorians.

- **Finally, a race of humans** called the Children of Mil invaded Ireland. They became the ancestors of the Celts.

- **When the Children of Mil** settled in Ireland, the Tuatha De Danaan used their magic powers to vanish from human sight, but have stayed in Ireland until this day.

◀ *Celtic tribes across Britain and Northern Europe worshipped a fearsome horned god who hunted human souls. One name for him was Cernunnos.*

Indian myths

◄ *The creator god Brahma is shown looking in all directions with four heads, to show that he has knowledge of all things.*

■ **Myths are still an important part** of Indian culture and religions today – as they have been for thousands of years.

■ **The earliest Indians** were farmers who thought that Prithivi, the earth, and Dyaus, the sky, were the parents of all gods and humans.

■ **A warrior race called the Aryans** then invaded India. They believed a god called Varuna created the world by picturing everything in his eye, the sun.

■ **Aryans believed that the storm god**, Indra, later took over as chief god, supported by human beings. He rearranged the universe by organizing the heavens and the seasons.

■ **The Hindu religion** grew from Aryan beliefs. Hindus believe that there is one great spirit called Brahman who is part of everything.

■ **There are three main gods** – Brahma, Vishnu and Shiva. They are thought to be three different forms of the great spirit Brahman.

■ **The god who creates** the world is Brahma. He emerges from a lotus flower floating on the floodwaters of chaos and creates everything simply by thinking of it.

■ **The god Vishnu preserves the balance** of good and evil in the universe. He protects the people of the world by becoming a human himself and resolving any problems that occur.

■ **The god Shiva** is the destroyer god. He combats demons and keeps the universe moving by dancing.

■ **After each 1000 Great Ages**, Shiva destroys the world by fire and flood. He preserves the seeds of all life in a golden egg, which Brahma breaks open to begin the rebirth of creation. Hindu mythology says the world is created, destroyed and recreated in cycles that continue forever.

◀ *Hindu families mark important stages in life, such as weddings, with prayers and religious ceremonies. They also believe that ordinary actions have religious meaning. Each good deed brings a person closer to their spiritual goal, which is freedom from life in this world and union with Brahman, the supreme god.*

Panku and Nugua Create the World

A Chinese myth

In the beginning, there was nothing but a giant egg. Inside the egg was a dark, dense, swirling mass of chaos. As the chaos subsided, a form began to take shape, growing into a dwarflike creature called Panku. Gradually, Panku began to breathe and his body tingled all over – he was alive. He opened his eyes and stretched – and found himself trapped in an egg, surrounded by dark, writhing forces. Panku struck out at the shell and burst the egg open. All the light contents, called Yin, rose over Panku and became the sky. All the heavy contents, called Yang, sank under Panku and became the earth.

As Panku tried to stand on the earth, he found that the sky was too low for him to straighten up. He set his hands against the sky above him and he planted his feet on the earth beneath him. Then Panku pushed and strained with all his might, until he forced the sky higher. At last, he could stretch out his body.

Panku realized that he would have to support the sky forever, or else it would fall and crush him. Day after day, he ate only mist. Night after night, he did not sleep. Each week Panku grew seventy feet, pushing the sky and the earth further away from each other. After eighteen thousand years, the sky and the earth were very far apart – so far apart that Panku thought it must surely be safe to lie down for a rest. He was extremely tired. At long last, Panku lowered his aching arms. He settled his stiff body on the earth, shut his weary eyelids and fell fast asleep.

Unfortunately, Panku never woke up. He died in his sleep, and his body became the world. His head and feet formed the sacred mountains of the east and west, his left and right arms formed the sacred mountains of the north and south, and his body formed the sacred mountain of the centre. Each sacred mountain towered out of the earth and acted as a mighty pillar to hold up the heavens. The hair on Panku's head became the planets and stars. His left eye became the sun, and his right eye became the moon. Panku's flesh became the earth's soil, while his bones and teeth became precious gems, minerals and metals. The hair on his body formed trees, plants and flowers. The fleas and fungi living on Panku's body developed into animals, birds, insects and fish. Oceans, rivers and streams were made from Panku's blood. Panku's breath became clouds and the wind, and his sweat became rain. Finally, Panku's voice formed lightning and thunder.

A goddess called Nugua caught sight of the wonderful world that had sprung from Panku's remains. She admired all its beauties, but she marvelled most at the creatures. She loved watching them feed and grow, living together in their communities.

Nugua decided to make her own miraculous creatures. She wanted hers to be better than any other living things and searched long and hard for materials to use. Swooping down from the sky, she scoured the golden shore. She tried using sand, but the figures crumbled. Then she tried rock, but it was too difficult to carve. Suddenly, her eyes spotted the thick mud of the Yellow River – perfect

modelling clay.
Scooping up handfuls of
wet clay, the great goddess
began patting, rolling, kneading
and pinching them into shape.

After many abandoned efforts, Nugua came up with a shape
that pleased her. She made more and more of the tiny figures and
thought up a name for them – people. She gave all her people
different heights and weights, but there were two basic types. One
type, she breathed Yang into and they became men. The other
type, she breathed Yin into and they became women. Nugua
clapped her hands with delight as the people began walking and
talking, and exploring their surroundings. The great goddess set

about making more people at once. She was so excited and impatient, she began wondering if there was a faster way to produce her children.

Nugua's eyes fell on a length of rope laying nearby. Grabbing the rope, she dangled it into the Yellow River mud. She rolled it around and around, until the end was covered with thick, sticky clay. Lifting it high, she shook it vigorously. Every drop that fell off became a new person. Nugua was thrilled. The people weren't as well formed as the ones she had made by hand – they were uglier and clumsier, and didn't have the same abilities and skills. However, Nugua didn't mind. It was a much faster method! Besides, she watched the two groups get to know each other and they seemed to get on quite well. The modelled people took charge of everyone and had good ideas, while the others were excellent workers and seemed quite comfortable being led. Everyone was happy …

The people built villages, dug wells, ploughed farmland, and generally made comfortable, ordered lives for themselves. Until one day, their activities disturbed a monster called Gong-gong who was asleep under the earth. Gong-gong awoke in a bad temper. He burst from the ground, leaving a river of fire pouring out of a vast crack in the earth. Throwing his head back, he roared and shook the soil from his shoulders. In a fit of rage, he reared up on his hind legs, headbutting one of the mountains that supported the sky. It crumbled and fell, tearing a great hole in the heavens. Waters gushed from the skies down onto the earth.

Nugua watched in horror as her people screamed and ran for their lives. Their homes were ablaze or washed away in torrents of water. The goddess acted quickly. Firstly, she set fire to the reeds that grew beside the Yellow River. Then she stuffed the ashes into the crack in the earth to stop the river of fire. She chose different coloured stones from the riverbed, and used them to patch up the tear in the sky.

With the fires dampened and the water washed away, the people began to return. Nugua smiled. Finally, her people were safe once more.

Who were the Maya?

■ **The Maya were a great race** who lived in modern-day Guatemala, Honduras and Yucatan, from 500 BC–AD 1524 when they were conquered by Spanish invaders.

■ **The Mayan creation story** is written in an ancient document called the Popol Vuh.

■ **As in the Christian creation story** in the Bible, the Popol Vuh says that women were created after men.

■ **The Maya believed** that in the beginning there was nothing but darkness, with sky above and sea below.

■ **Myths say that a group of gods** shaped the landscape and formed animals and birds.

■ **The Popol Vuh explains** that the first two human races made by the creators were not good enough and had to be destroyed. The first people were mindless, made from clay. The second people were soulless, made from wood.

■ **The first successful people** were made out of corn, at the suggestion of a jaguar, coyote, crow and parrot.

■ **The third race of humans** were thought to be so perfect that they were almost as good as the creators themselves. The creators clouded the intelligence of the humans so they could no longer see the gods, and could only see things that were close to them.

■ **By eating certain plants and herbs**, the Maya thought they would be able to see the gods again and cheat the curse of the creators.

■ **The Maya believed that the world** was in complete darkness when human beings were created. People begged for some light, so the creators made the sun, moon and stars.

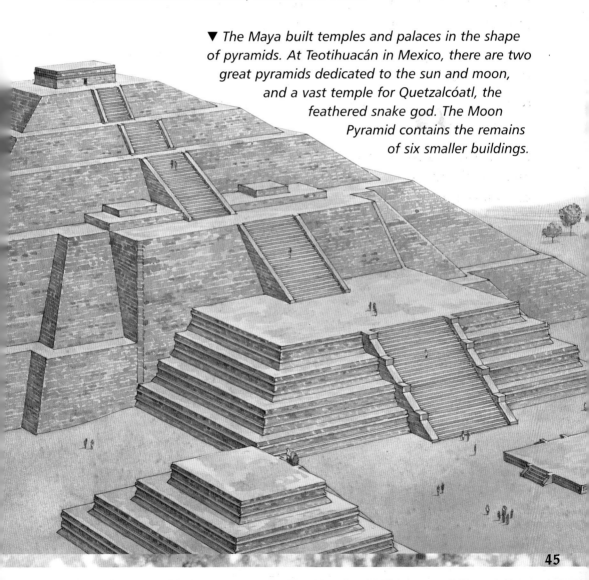

▼ *The Maya built temples and palaces in the shape of pyramids. At Teotihuacán in Mexico, there are two great pyramids dedicated to the sun and moon, and a vast temple for Quetzalcóatl, the feathered snake god. The Moon Pyramid contains the remains of six smaller buildings.*

Toltec and Aztec tales

■ **The Toltecs were a great civilization** in Mexico from AD 900–1200. The Aztecs were a race of warriors who came to power in 1376. Their first ruler claimed to be a descendant of the chief Toltec god, and so they adopted Toltec myths and legends.

■ **The Toltecs built** huge pyramid temples that still stand, covered in pictures telling their myths.

■ **Aztec myths were recorded** on an ancient Aztec calendar, and on a document explaining how Aztec gods fit into the calendar.

■ **The Toltecs and Aztecs believed** that both humans and the gods needed to make sacrifices in order to keep the universe alive.

■ **In the beginning**, the gods created and destroyed four worlds one after another because humans did not make enough sacrifices.

■ **In order to create a sun** for the fifth world, two gods sacrificed themselves by jumping into a flaming bonfire.

■ **At first, the fifth world consisted** only of water with a female monster goddess floating in it, eating everything. The mighty gods Quetzalcóatl and Tezcatlipoca turned her body into the earth and the heavens.

◄ *The name Quetzalcóatl means 'feathered serpent'. His statue is found carved into many ancient sites in Central America.*

▲ *The Toltec ruins, known today as El Castillo, date from the 11th century AD. A stepped pyramid, this temple was used to worship the god Quetzalcóatl.*

■ **The Aztecs believed** that the sun god and the earth monster needed sacrifices of human blood and hearts in order to remain fertile and alive.

■ **Humans were created** by Quetzalcóatl from the powdered bones of his dead father and his own blood.

■ **Quetzalcóatl and Tezcatlipoca brought** musicians and singers from the House of the Sun down to earth. From then on, every living thing could create its own kind of music.

South American stories

- **Most South American myths** come from the Inca race, who built a great empire in Peru from the 13th century AD until they were conquered by Spanish invaders in 1532.

- **Inca means 'children of the sun'.** Some South American myths say that the sun was created on an island in Lake Titicaca.

- **Inca mythology grew from ancient tales** told by tribal peoples who lived in Peru from around 2500 BC.

- **A pre-Inca Tiahuanaco myth tells** that in the beginning a god called Con Ticci Viracocha emerged out of nothingness and created everything.

- **Con Ticci Viracocha is said** to have returned to earth out of Lake Titicaca, destroyed his world in a huge flood, and then created everything again.

- **Another myth tells how the first humans** were created by a boneless man called Con, the son of the sun. He was later overthrown by another child of the sun, Pachacamac, who created a new race of people.

▲ *This statue was created by the Tiahuanaco people of Peru. This important civilization lived in the highlands around Lake Titicaca before the Incas invaded.*

■ **An ancient coastal tribe in Peru believed** in a creator god called Coniraya. He filled the sea with fish and taught them how to farm the land.

■ **The Canaris tribe thought** that they were descended from an ancient parrot or macaw that had bred with the few survivors of a terrible flood.

■ **Inca mythology tells** that the Incas magically appeared one day from a place called Paccari-tambo, which means 'inn of origin'.

■ **Myths say that the first Incas** were led by eight royal gods – four brothers and four sisters.

▼ *These modern-day Peruvians are fishing on Lake Titicaca – an important site in Inca myth.*

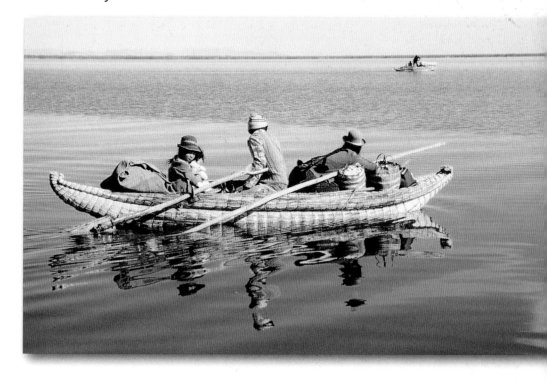

The Children of the Sun

An ancient Peruvian myth

L ong, long ago, people lived like wild animals. They had no homes and had to shelter in mountain caves and forest hollows. They had no clothes, so covered themselves in scraps of animal skin and tree bark, or they went naked and barefoot. They could not grow their own food and had to find food in the forest. Sometimes they gathered berries, nuts and fruits to eat; other times they hunted animals, birds and fish.

Every day, the great father – the sun – travelled across the sky and watched what was happening on earth. He provided heat, for the people's comfort and health; he provided light, so they could see and gain knowledge; he made sure that plants grew and animals thrived, providing food. Yet he was dismayed at what he saw. "My people do not know how to live properly," the sun sighed. "They haven't built houses or villages. They have no manners or laws. They don't use tools or utensils. They don't have clothes or belongings. They don't even tend to flocks or herds. They don't know how to worship the gods and ask us for help."

The sun thought hard about what he could do. Finally, he decided. "My divine sons and daughters could teach these people how to behave, just as I have taught them. I must send one son and one daughter down to these pitiful creatures to teach them how to improve their lives."

The sun chose Manco Capac from his sons and Mama Ocllo Huaco from his daughters. "I am sending you down to earth at Lake Titicaca," the sun instructed his children. "I am making you the rulers of all the people there. They are living savagely and shamefully, and they cannot help themselves. I want you to show them how things should be done. Guide them with justice and love, just as I have done for you." The sun handed Manco Capac and Mama Ocllo Huaco a golden rod, decorated with intricate patterns. "Take this," he commanded. "It will help you find the area where the soil is the most fertile. Wherever you travel, thrust the rod into the earth and see if it sinks in entirely. If it does, that is the place to stop and settle. I want you to establish a sacred city there. Call it Cuzco – the city of the sun."

Manco Capac and Mama Ocllo Huaco dressed in their finest, most brightly coloured, highly patterned woollen robes. They adorned themselves with gleaming golden earrings, bracelets and necklaces. Then they left the heavens and descended to earth at Lake Titicaca, as their father had instructed.

The children of the sun travelled far and wide over the land, climbing the highest mountains against the might of the wind, hacking through deep, overgrown gorges, and hiking over featureless plains in the heat and humidity. In every area, they tried to thrust the rod into the earth – but the ground remained firm and unyielding.

Finally, Manco Capac and Mama Ocllo Huaco climbed to the top of a hill, where lush, green valleys lay all around. There, Manco Capac drew out the golden rod and held it aloft. With one swift downward blow, he thrust it into the earth. To his delight, the golden rod sank into the soil and disappeared completely.

"This is where our beloved father intends us to build his sacred city," announced Manco Capac eagerly.

"Let us go into the surrounding valleys," agreed Mama Ocllo Huaco. "We will gather the people and bring them to this place, where we will care for them and teach them, just as our father has cared for and taught us."

The people of the area were in awe of the impressive appearance and noble attitude of Manco Capac and Mama Ocllo Huaco. They cowered into submission and listened meekly to their message.

"Follow us and we will teach you how to live a better life," explained the children of the sun. "We will show you how to build homes, how to make clothes, and how to raise animals and plants for food. We will show you how to worship the sun, the mighty father of us all, who has sent us here to help you." And the enthralled people followed Manco Capac and Mama Ocllo Huaco to the site that would become their new home.

The children of the sun set about teaching the people new skills. Firstly, Manco Capac and Mama Ocllo Huaco showed them which foods were both tasty and nourishing. They explained the secrets of the seasons and the weather. In spring, the people learnt how to choose the best seeds, how to plant them, and how to raise crops. They were then shown how to make tools and equipment needed for farming. Wild animals were tamed and set to work. Cattle, sheep and chickens were herded to be raised for food or supplies, such as wool. Next, the children of the sun helped them to build great villages. After explaining about building materials and techniques, the people began building homes and organizing the society with guidelines and laws. They set up systems to provide water for the land and people's homes. The people were shown important skills, such as weaving, sewing and shoe making. To defend their community if attacked, the people learnt how to make weapons and how to fight. Lastly, the children of the sun organized the building of a temple on the spot at the top of the hill where they had buried the golden rod. The people began to worship the sun with offerings and sacrifices, learning how to respect and please the gods.

And so it was that Manco Capac and Mama Ocllo Huaco founded a great nation. The people of Lake Titicaca had become civilized and educated, just as the great father, the sun, had wished. From then on, they called themselves the Incas – the chosen children of the sun.

Early Japanese myths

■ **The earliest people to live in Japan** were called the Ainu. They believed that in the beginning the world was a swampy mixture of water and earth where nothing lived.

■ **According to Ainu myth**, a creator god called Kamui sent a water wagtail to the swamp. By fluttering its wings and tail, islands appeared from the water.

■ **The Ainu believed** that people and animals were created by Kamui to live on the islands.

■ **During the second and first centuries** BC, people from Asia arrived in Japan. They brought a nature religion called Shinto with them.

■ **According to Shinto myths**, the world was at first an ocean of chaos, which gradually divided into light heavens above and heavy earth below.

◄ *In the religion of Shinto, priests make offerings to the spirits of nature. They believe that all things that inspire awe in the natural world have* kami *(spirits).*

■ **The first god was thought to be** like a reed shoot that grew in the space between heaven and earth.

■ **A female god called Izanami** and a male god called Izanagi gave shape to the world. They stood on a rainbow and Izanagi stirred the ocean with a spear. An island formed, and the two gods left heaven to go and live on it.

■ **The Shinto myth** says that Japan was formed when Izanami gave birth to eight children who became islands.

■ **Izanami and Izanagi had many other children**. These were the gods that shaped and then lived in every aspect of nature – the winds, seas, rivers, trees and mountains.

■ **The ruler of the universe** is the sun goddess, Amaterasu. She was born from Izanagi's left eye.

◀ *The Shinto religion has traditional dances, dating from AD 400. They are performed to religious chanting and accompanied by the rhythmic beating of huge drums.*

Izanami and Izanagi Create a Great Country

A Japanese myth

*I*n the beginning, the universe was a swirling mass of matter. Gradually, the lighter matter rose up and became the heavens. The heavier matter sank down and became the oceans. A void existed between the two, in which a being formed – it looked like a reed shoot when it sprouts out of mud. This being was the first god. The god floated in the void as a cloud floats over the sea. Over time, other gods also began to form. The two youngest were a male called Izanagi No Mikoto and a female called Izanami No Mikoto.

Izanagi and Izanami looked down on the watery wastes beneath them. "I wonder if there is something down there for us to stand upon," pondered Izanami.

Izanagi plunged his spear into the ocean, to see if it hit anything solid. He moved the spear this way and that way in the depths, testing the waters. When he withdrew the spear, droplets of salty sea water fell from its tip and formed an island.

"Now we have land to rest on," he exclaimed eagerly. "We can go and live down there among the waters."

Izanagi and Izanami descended to earth on the bridge from the heavens – a rainbow. Firstly, they made their island beautiful with trees and flowers. Then, they thrust Izanagi's spear into the centre

of the island and built a large palace around it. One day, they caught sight of two wagtails flying through the trees together, chirping happily. Izanagi and Izanami realized the secret of making new life. They hoped to create many children of their own – more islands – which would join together to form a great country.

Izanagi and Izanami held a marriage ceremony. They performed a sacred ritual, in which they each travelled around the island in opposite directions until they met and greeted each other politely.

"Good day, handsome young man," said Izanami.

"Good day, beautiful young woman," replied Izanagi.

In due course, Izanami gave birth to their first child. However, instead of being a beautiful island, it was misshapen, ugly and infertile. Izanagi and Izanami were horrified. This was not what they had in mind at all. Disappointed, they set it adrift on the ocean, and decided to start again.

The two gods hurried up to heaven to seek advice from the older, wiser gods. "Why did we have an abnormal child?" they asked. "Is there anything we can do to stop us having more?"

The gods shook their heads and pointed sternly at Izanami. "She gave birth to a useless offspring because she does not know her proper place," they scolded. "Women should allow men to speak first," they warned, "or else there will be bad luck."

Izanagi and Izanami glided back down to their island to try again. They performed the sacred ritual once more, travelling around the island in opposite directions until they met and greeted each other politely. This time, Izanagi spoke first.

"Good day, beautiful young woman," he said.

"Good day, handsome young man," Izanami replied.

In due course, Izanami gave birth to eight children. They were all beautiful islands. Together, they formed the country of Japan.

At first, Izanagi and Izanami were thrilled. After a while, the gods began to grumble because the islands were covered in mists. "What is the point in creating a wonderful country if no one can see it?"

Izanagi drew up all his breath and then blew out as hard as he could. Another child flew from him – the god of the wind. The god of the wind blew away the mists from the islands. Delighted, Izanagi and Izanami set about creating other gods to make the islands perfect. They created the gods of the seas to ensure that blue waters lapped the shores, the gods of the mountains to raise lofty peaks towards the heavens, the gods of the rivers to bring life-giving waterfalls and springs, and the gods of the trees, plants and flowers to form shady forests, fruit-filled orchards and fragrant meadows.

The next child born to Izanagi and Izanami was the god of fire. However, when he was being born, he burned Izanami so badly that she died. Her spirit fled into Yomi, the underworld.

Izanagi was grief-stricken. In his agony, he struck off the baby's head, causing several gods to spring forth. Then he set off down the long path that led to the dark realm of the dead. He was determined to find Izanami and bring her back to the land of the living.

Izanagi searched the cold, dark underworld for his beloved wife. However, by the time he discovered Izanami, her body had begun to rot, as she had eaten Yomi's food and belonged to the underworld forever. Izanagi was horrified.

Izanami was humiliated that her husband had seen her terrible state. "My husband, you must accept my death," she roared, surrounded by howling demons. "We have loved each other and created a beautiful country with many gods. Now we must agree to part for ever more."

Realizing that Izanami was right, Izanagi returned to Japan and performed rituals to wash away the taint of death. First, Izanagi bathed in a river on the island of Kyushu. This created many evil demons, but Izanagi created gods to fight and control them. Then

Izanagi washed in the sea. Bathing his left eye, he created Amaterasu, the brilliant goddess of the sun. Bathing his right eye, he created Tsukiyomi, the shining god of the moon. Amaterasu and Tsukiyomi lived in the heavens, lighting up the entire world. When Izanagi bathed his nose, he created Susano, the god of storms. Susano was troublesome, wreaking havoc and destruction, so Izanagi banished him to live in the underworld with his mother. Before Susano left, he visited his sister Amaterasu in the heavens. Susano gave Amaterasu his sword, which she chewed and then breathed forth three goddesses. Amaterasu gave Susano her five-strand necklace, which he chewed and then breathed forth five gods. From these eight gods, the children of the sun, descended a great race of nobles. They became the emperors of Japan.

Tales from Africa

■ **Numerous tribal groups** have lived in Africa for thousands of years, all with their own different myths and legends, although many shared beliefs.

■ **Most African tribes** believe in one supreme creator god and many minor gods.

■ **Different tribal names** for the creator god include Mulungu, Leza, Amma and Nyambe.

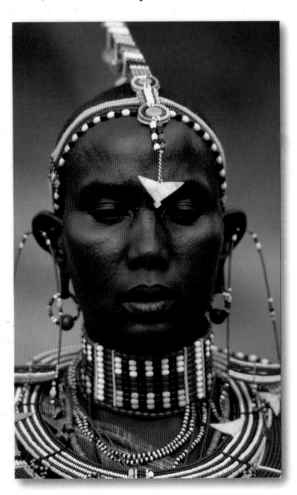

■ **Many myths** say that the creator god grew weary of the constant demands from the people, so he left the earth and went to live in heaven.

◄ *The Maasai tribe of East Africa worship their creator god, Ngai. The women wear an elaborate display of beads. Blue represents god and the sky, and green is for god's greatest blessing, the grass.*

▶ *According to legends from central Africa, the hero Chibinda Ilunga was the prince of the Luba people. After falling in love with Lweji, a Lunda princess, he ruled over her nation wisely.*

■ **The Yoruba people of Nigeria** believed that in the beginning the universe was made up of the sky, ruled by the chief god Olorun, and a watery marshland, ruled by the goddess Olokun.

■ **The Yoruba believed that the god** Obatala shaped the earth with the help of magic gifts from other gods.

■ **The Fon people of Benin** believed that the world was created by twin gods – the moon goddess Mawu, and her twin brother Lisa, the sun.

■ **The Dogon people of Mali** believed that the creator god moulded the sun, moon, earth and humans out of clay.

■ **The Pygmies believed** that the first man and woman were released from a tree in a gush of water by a chameleon.

■ **The Yoruba believed** that the chief god Olorun breathed life into the first people, who were modelled from mud.

Obatala Creates Life

A west African myth

At the start of the universe, there was only endless sky above, and misty waters below. The only living things were gods and goddesses. There was no vegetation, no animals, and no people. The sky was ruled by the supreme being, the god Olorun. The wastelands were ruled by a powerful goddess, Olokun.

One day, a young god called Obatala looked down from the heavens and thought that the foggy, swampy world was terribly empty. He went to see the wise Olorun. "Have you thought of creating solid land?" Obatala suggested. "It could look wonderfully varied with all sorts of bright colours. There could be mountains and valleys, forests and fields, rivers and waterfalls. Animals could live together in the wilderness, feeding on the fruits of nature. Then we could create people – creatures who look like us – and they could thrive in great communities."

"That is an excellent idea," agreed Olorun, "but who knows how to make the world like this?"

"Allow me to find out," urged Obatala, and he eagerly set off on his challenge.

Obatala went to see Olorun's eldest son, Orunmila, who had the gift of seeing into the future.

"Your father has given me permission to create solid land and creatures to live on it," Obatala explained. "Can you see how I may achieve this?"

Gazing thoughtfully into the distance, Orunmila announced, "You will need a chain of gold, long enough to reach from the endless sky above to the misty waters below. You must fill a snail's shell with sand. Then put the shell in a bag, along with a white hen, a black cat and a palm nut. Take the bag and climb down the chain to the watery wastelands."

In turn, Obatala went to see every god and goddess in the heavens. One by one, he described his plan for creation to them, and begged them to donate their gold to make a chain. Fortunately, Obatala won over each of the divine beings. They gave him all the gold they possessed, and soon Obatala had collected a huge treasure trove of gold earrings, gold bracelets, and gold rings. Obatala loaded the sacks of gold onto his chariot and hurried to the workshop of the god's goldsmith.

The goldsmith shook his head and sighed. "I do not think that will be enough to make the chain as long as you wish, but I will do my best." And with that, he set to work at once.

While the goldsmith clanged and banged in his fiery forge, Obatala collected the other items Orunmila had mentioned. Then, when the chain was finished, Orunmila helped Obatala fasten one

end to the edge of the sky, and
let the rest fall far below. Embracing Orunmila
in farewell, Obatala took his bag, and began to climb down
the golden chain.

Down, down and down he went, until he descended into the
mists and felt spray from the waters below wetting his legs. Then
came a faint voice from above him. It was Orunmila. "Sprinkle the
sand from your snail shell," the god shouted down. Reaching into
his bag, Obatala took out the shell, and sprinkled the sand down
upon the waters. Then came Orunmila's voice again. "Now release
the white hen." Again, Obatala did as he was told. The white hen
fluttered down to the sandy waters and scratched away. The sand
spread and formed dry land in all directions, as far as Obatala
could see.

Finally, there was something solid for Obatala to land upon.
However, as the goldsmith had feared, the chain did not quite
reach down far enough. Dangling from the final golden link, he
took a deep breath, and jumped, landing safely on the soft earth.
Pleased with his creation, Obatala named the place Ilé-Ifé. Taking
the palm nut from his bag, he carefully buried it in the ground. It
sprouted immediately, springing up into a towering palm tree.

Nuts from its strong branches
dropped to the ground, and they shot up into fully
grown trees, too. Soon, there was a shady forest all around. Finally,
Obatala used some of the palm trunks and leaves to build himself
a house. Then he took the black cat out of his bag to keep him
company in his new home.

The great ruler Olorun looked down from the sky and was
delighted to see what Obatala had achieved. However, he noticed
that the young god was living in gloomy twilight. It seemed very
unpleasant, compared to the brightness of the heavens. Olorun
created a ball of brilliance, the sun, and hung it in the sky
to give Obatala cheering light and warmth every day.

Although pleased with his surroundings, Obatala
had not finished his creation yet. He scooped up
some clay and began modelling little figures to
look just like him. The sun baked down as
Obatala worked, making him hot and thirsty. The
young god drank bowl after bowl of palm wine,
without realizing that it was making him drunk!
The last few figures he made were not as good as
the earlier ones. They were misshapen – with
long arms and legs – but Obatala was too drunk
to notice. When he was happy with the number

of figures he had before him, Obatala called up to the supreme being. "Help me, oh great Olorun, by breathing life into these figures so they may become people."

And so the figures woke up and lived. When Obatala's drunkenness wore off, he was very sad that his people were not perfect. He promised to be their special protector for ever more. Obatala helped them to make houses, and to farm the land. The people called themselves the Yoruba and Ilé-Ifé became a prosperous village, then a mighty city.

When Obatala saw that his people were thriving, he climbed back up the golden chain into the sky. From then on, he lived sometimes with the other gods in the heavens, and sometimes with his people on earth.

Greeks and Romans

■ **The Romans and Greeks worshipped** many supreme beings. The gods and goddesses of ancient Greece were adopted by the Romans, under new names. For example, Zeus became Jove and Poseidon became Neptune.

■ **The stories about Greek and Roman gods**, spirits and heroes are known as classical mythology.

■ **Unlike Greek mythology**, Roman beliefs focus on the heroism of humans, such as Aeneas, rather than only the gods.

▼ *The Parthenon in Greece was a temple built to honour the goddess Athene. Above the entrance, the triangular pediments show scenes from Greek myths.*

▶ *The ancient Romans made offerings to the gods in a shrine. The shrine contained statues of ancient gods called lares and penates. Lares were ancestor spirits, and penates guarded the family's food.*

■ **Myths say that giants** called the Cyclopes gave gifts to the gods. Zeus was given the gift of thunder and lightning, and Poseidon received a trident, with which he could stir up sea-storms and tidal waves.

■ **The gods, except for Artemis**, the hunter goddess, opposed human sacrifice and cannibalism. Zeus once punished King Lycaon for eating human flesh by turning him into a wolf.

■ **The Greek gods and goddesses** sometimes fell in love with humans. Zeus fell in love with Alcmene, and they had a son, the hero Heracles.

■ **In Greece, the Golden Age** was a time when the gods and men lived together on earth. When men became cruel, the gods left for the heavens.

■ **The ancient Greeks and Romans** believed that spirits called dryads lived inside trees. According to myth, Apollo once fell in love with the dryad, Daphne. To escape him, she turned herself into a laurel tree.

■ **The word temple comes from** the Latin, *templum*, meaning the area where a shrine to a god was erected.

■ **Greeks and Romans** would leave small offerings, such as food or flowers, at the shrines of the gods. They believed that this would appease the gods, which would in turn give them a better life.

The Titans

- **The Titans** were 12 immortals in Greek and Roman mythology.

- **The cleverest Titan** was Prometheus. However, when he stole fire from the gods to give to the humans, he was punished by Zeus.

- **A Titan called Epimetheus** married the first mortal woman, Pandora. According to myth, Pandora opened a forbidden box, unleashing evil upon the world.

- **The Titan Helios** became the god of the sun, Selene became the goddess of the moon, and Rhea became an earth goddess.

- **Oceanus became the god** of the river that the Greeks believed surrounded the earth.

- **Themis became the goddess** of prophecies at the city Delphi.

- **A prophecy said that the youngest Titan**, Cronus, would be overthrown by his own son. So when Cronus' children were born, he ate them. However, his wife hid one child away – this was Zeus.

◄ *The wise Titan Prometheus helped the human race by teaching mortals special skills.*

▶ *After the war between the gods and the Titans, the god Zeus punished the strongest Titan Atlas by commanding him to hold up the skies on his shoulders.*

■ **When Zeus** was grown up, he fed Cronus a cup of poison, causing him to bring up all the other children he had swallowed – the gods and goddesses Poseidon, Hades, Hera, Demeter and Hestia.

■ **Zeus fought with his brothers** and sisters against the Titans for ten years. The Titans were finally overthrown when the gods and goddesses secured the help of the hundred-handed giants and the Cyclopes.

■ **The Titans were hurled into an underworld realm** of punishment called Tartarus. There, they were bound in chains forever.

The Rebellious Titans and Gods

A Greek myth

Before the beginning of time, there was nothing but an emptiness called Chaos. Out of the darkness emerged three beings who became known as Gaea, Tartarus and Eros.

Gaea, the earth goddess wished for some company, so she gave birth to Uranus, the god of the sky, and he surrounded her on all sides. Next, the mountains and the sea sprang from Gaea, shaping the landscape of the world.

Soon, Gaea and Uranus created three children together – giants, each with fifty heads and one hundred arms! Shortly after, three more children were born to them – again giants. But this time, they each had just one eye in the middle of their forehead. They came to be known as the Cyclopes.

With such immense strength and power, Uranus became fearful that the children would eventually try to overthrow him and take control of the universe themselves. So one by one, Uranus seized them, throwing them down into the depths of Tartarus, the underworld, from where they could not possibly threaten him.

Furious and devastated, Gaea began to hate Uranus for his cold-hearted, ruthless actions. With time, she gave birth to thirteen more children – the immortal Titans. Among them were the god of the sun Helios, the goddess of the moon Selene, the god of the waters Oceanus, the goddess of prophecy Themis, the strongest Titan Atlas, and finally Prometheus – the most intelligent Titan, who created the human race out of soft clay.

Yet Gaea's bitterness towards Uranus only increased with time. The day came when she put a mighty, curved sickle into the hands of her youngest Titan son, Cronus. "I want to punish your cruel father and free your brothers and sisters from their underground banishment," she explained. "If you kill your father, you can rule in his place."

His eyes gleaming greedily, Cronus did what he was told. Across the universe echoed his father's cries of agony. Rivers of blood flowed from his wounds, and from this stream of wickedness sprang forth three evil creatures, the Furies, and a race of terrifying warrior giants.

Being immortal, Uranus couldn't die, so Cronus threw his father's body into the ocean. "Now I reign over all things!" Cronus roared.

To Gaea's despair, Cronus proved to be just as much of a tyrant as her husband. Relishing his control over the universe, he refused to free the hundred-handed giants and the Cyclopes from Tartarus.

Outraged, Gaea warned, "Your cruelty will come full circle! The day will come when your children will destroy you, just as you have destroyed your own father."

Cronus simply sneered. In his arrogance, he thought that he could cheat the prophecy. He would make sure that he had no children. If he had none, then how could they vanquish him?

Cronus was married to his sister, Rhea. In due course, a baby daughter Hestia was born. Cronus didn't hesitate in swallowing her whole. To Rhea's horror and misery, Cronus did exactly the same with their next four babies – Demeter, Hera, Hades and Poseidon. By the time Rhea was due to give birth to their fifth child, her heart was breaking with grief. She went to Gaea and begged for help. "Mother," she sobbed, "how can I fool Cronus, so I can keep my baby? I can't stand to lose another!"

Gaea eagerly came up with a plan. She hid Rhea away in a mountainside cave on the island of Crete. There, unseen, Rhea gave birth to a baby boy called Zeus. Rhea left Zeus in Gaea's care, and hurried home. Then she wrapped a rock in a blue blanket and presented it to Cronus. "Here is your newborn son!" she proclaimed. Cronus didn't spare a second to look at the infant. He simply opened his jaws and gulped the bundle down. Smirking with satisfaction, he thought of how he had defeated his destiny once again …

And so, unknown to his father, Zeus grew up safely into a

strong, courageous god. When he came of age, he disguised himself as one of Cronus' servants and waited. Then, when one day Cronus called for a drink to be brought to him, the disguised Zeus carefully took him a chalice of sweet-tasting poison instead. In one gulp, Cronus drained the drink – and immediately realized that something was wrong. Clutching and clawing at his stomach, cramps and spasms stabbed inside him. Suddenly, up came the rock he had swallowed, followed by Poseidon, Hades, Hera, Demeter and Hestia – who were all fully grown … and furious!

"Behold your son, Zeus, and all your other children!" Rhea said proudly. "They are ready to rule in your place, with justice and wisdom, instead of cruelty and tyranny. Your fate has come!"

"You will regret this because this means war!" bellowed Cronus, striding away to prepare for battle.

While Cronus was rousing all the other Titans to fight at his side, Zeus sped down to Tartarus with his brothers and sisters to release the hundred-handed giants and the Cyclopes. Of course, the monsters were so grateful that they immediately pledged their allegiance to the gods and goddesses and vowed to fight with them. Then the Cyclopes presented Zeus and his brothers with special gifts to help them in their mighty task. To Zeus, they gave the weapons of thunder and lightning. To Poseidon, they gave a magic trident for stirring up sea-storms and creating earthquakes. To Hades, they gave a helmet of invisibility.

It was now time for the gods and goddesses to return to the upper world and begin the battle for the universe. Enraged, the Titans were ready and waiting, forming a formidable flank behind Cronus. With blood-curdling war cries, they flung themselves forwards across the heavens into the attack.

As the Titans advanced, the hundred-handed giants tore great chunks of rock off the mountains and hurled them at the enemy. The two sides clashed together, in an embroiled mass of arrows, spears and swords. The blows of the mighty warriors made the earth tremble and shake until the awful rumblings were heard down in the depths of Tartarus itself. The cries and groans of the injured echoed around the mountains and across the heavens. And still the Titans and the gods fought, inflicting terrible wounds on each other. As immortals, none of them could die.

When Zeus unleashed his ear-splitting thunderclaps and blinding lightning bolts, the stench of smouldering flesh filled the air as the Titans were set alight. While the Titans threw themselves into the sea, trying to quench the burning flames, the hundred-handed giants saw their chance. Seizing the howling Titans one by one, the giants dragged them below the earth down to the underworld. There, they bound them in the strongest of chains and left them for all eternity.

How the victorious gods and goddesses rejoiced! At last, tyranny had been overthrown and they would rule together, spreading fairness and heroism throughout the universe. The gods decided upon their kingdoms – Hades won the underworld and became the king of the dead. Poseidon won the sea and became lord of the oceans. And Zeus won the sky, and became ruler of the world. All three leaders determined not only to keep peace and harmony among immortal beings, but also to teach humans how to live prosperous lives – to respect their fellow people, all other living creatures, and above all, the gods themselves.

Contented, the gods and goddesses made their own home on Mount Olympus. And there they have ruled ever since.

Norse warrior gods

■ **Ancient Norse peoples** told stories about a race of gods and goddesses called the Aesir. They were brave warriors, just like the Vikings themselves.

■ **Odin, the chief of the warrior gods**, has a high throne called Lidskialf, from which he can see anything happening in the universe.

■ **Odin occasionally likes** to disguise himself as a traveller and wander undetected through the world of humans.

■ **Norse gods and goddesses** are not immortal. According to one legend, Odin's son, Baldur, was accidentally killed by a piece of mistletoe.

■ **The most important warrior goddesses** are Odin's wife, Frigg, a mother goddess with fertility powers, and the beautiful Freya, the goddess of love.

■ **The daughters of Odin** were beautiful spirits called the Valkyries. They took brave warriors who had died in battle to live happily in a hall called Valhalla in Asgard.

■ **The Aesir** (warrior gods) once fought against the Vanir (fertility gods). They finally made a peaceful alliance against the giants.

■ **The son of Odin and Frigg**, Tyr, was the god of war. He is often regarded as the one-handed god because the monstrous wolf, Fenris, bit his hand off.

■ **The ruler of the Vanir** was the fertility god Njord, ruler of the winds and the sea.

■ **Two days of the week** are named after Norse warrior gods. Wednesday means Woden's Day – Woden was another name for Odin, the father of the gods. Thursday means Thor's Day, after the Norse god of thunder.

▼ Norse stories are the mythology of the Vikings – seafaring warriors from Norway, Sweden and Denmark who invaded other parts of Europe.

The gods of Egypt

■ **The mighty sun god**, Ra, was called many different names by the ancient Egyptians.

■ **The young sun god, Khepri**, was sometimes pictured as a scarab beetle. This is because a scarab beetle rolls a ball of dung before it, as the sun rolls across the sky like a ball.

■ **Myths say that the sun god** has a secret name, known only to himself, which was the key to all his power.

■ **The ancient Egyptians** believed that part of the god's spirit could live on earth in the body of an animal. This is why their gods are pictured as humans with animal heads.

■ **Hathor or Sekhmet** was the daughter and wife of Ra. She could take on the form of a terrifying lioness or cobra to attack and punish enemies of the sun god.

■ **The son of Ra** was Osiris. He became king of Egypt and later, ruler of the underworld.

■ **Osiris' brother**, Seth, represented evil in the universe. He hatched a wicked plot to murder Osiris and take the crown of Egypt for himself.

■ **The powerful mother goddess of fertility** was Isis, Osiris' sister and wife.

◄ *The blue scarab beetle of Khepri is one of the many forms of the sun god.*

▼ *Osiris, king of Egypt, wears the white crown of Egypt, and carries a crook and flail. The crook, shaped like a shepherd's staff, symbolized government, while the flail showed the power of the pharaoh. Osiris' son, Horus, is depicted with the head of a falcon. The goddess, Isis, carries the ankh symbol, the sign of life.*

■ **Horus was Osiris' son**. He inherited the throne of Egypt. Ancient Egyptians believed that all pharaohs were descended from Horus, and therefore they were gods.

■ **An amulet is a piece of jewellery** with magical powers. Many amulets were in the shape of an eye – either of the sun god or Horus. The sacred eye was thought to have healing powers and was able to ward off evil.

Ra's Secret Name

An ancient Egyptian myth

Before time began, nothing existed except an endless dark ocean of chaos. Forming himself out of this nothing, the creator then made a world in the middle of the ocean. He lit the world with his own brilliance – the light of the sun, and then made other gods and goddesses to keep him company. Next came the humans, to be his children.

Every day, the creator sailed across the sky in a boat of blazing light, surveying the world. Each evening, his sun boat sank, into the underworld. Using his powers to protect himself from the clutches of the dead, he journeyed through their kingdom to fight the evils. Every morning, he sailed safely back up into the sky.

Out of all the other gods and goddesses, Isis was the strongest. Clever and cunning, she made it her business to become the wisest

of them all. Patiently, she travelled all over the world, discovering the hidden properties of everything the creator had made. Eventually, she knew millions of spells and secrets – except for one. She did not know the secret name of the creator himself – the root to all his power.

Isis was well aware that Ra would never give up his secret name, unless he was forced. However, Isis also knew that nothing could harm Ra – his spirit of creation was far too strong for that.

Isis thought long and hard. She realized that Ra could only be affected by something from his own body. But even if she could get hold of a strand of hair or a flake of his skin, how could she make a dangerous weapon?

Biding her time, one day, Isis saw her opportunity. Sometimes, Ra would leave his sun-boat in the heavens and descend down to earth on foot. On such a walk, Ra paused to talk to a group of gods. Suddenly, Isis saw a drop of spittle fall from his mouth. As swift as the wind, she caught the spittle and whisked herself away.

Hidden in her palace, Isis mixed the spittle of the mighty Ra with some earth, making clay. Muttering words of strong magic, she shaped the clay into the form of a snake. Then, closing her eyes, Isis carefully spoke the secret words of creation.

The great goddess stood back and watched. It was only a moment before bright colours wrapped themselves all around the clay creature from the tip of its nose to the point of its tail. With a wriggle, the snake reared its head and opened its eyes, hissing and flickering its forked tongue. It was alive.

Isis clapped her hands with delight, her eyes shining. Cautiously, she picked up the creature and carried it to a spot on one of Ra's favourite walks. Staring deep into its eyes, she whispered its instructions, then let it ripple away across the earth. As the snake found a shady hiding place and disappeared from view, Isis hurried away into the shadows.

That very day, Ra happened to stroll along that way, admiring the beauty of his creation. Suddenly, without warning, he received a terrible shock. He felt something he had never felt before – pain. Screaming in agony, he collapsed to the ground, clutching his foot. In his pain, he did not notice a strange snake slithering away from him – Isis' snake.

Ra howled as burning poison began to spread through his flesh. Hearing the cries of the great creator, the other gods and goddesses came running to him in alarm.

"Something has hurt me! I didn't see it and I cannot guess what it might have been, for nothing I have made can hurt me!" the creator gasped. "Help me!" Ra begged, growing pale and sweating. "I fear that I am dying."

Panicking, the gods and goddesses tried all the magic they knew, making every desperate effort they could think of to heal the creator. Nothing made any difference. Ra shook as the poison began to stiffen his muscles

Then, Isis stepped forward. "Great father," she said, her voice filled with fake concern, "I think I know a spell that could save you – but it will only work if I use your secret name."

Ra groaned – not only in pain, but also in horror. He had no choice. Summoning all his remaining energy, he feebly beckoned Isis to bend down close to him. The goddess struggled to contain her excitement, and put her ear to the creator's lips.

"I will tell you my secret name," Ra murmured, his breathing becoming shallow. "But only if you never reveal it to anyone."

"I promise!" Isis agreed, eagerly.

At last, Isis had the power she wanted. She healed Ra as the other gods and goddesses stood back in awe of her incredible magic. Fully restored, Ra rose through the heavens into his sunboat, and light shone down on the world once more.

Native American spirits

■ **By using legends**, Native Americans tried to trace their ancestors back to a particular animal or bird. They made carvings called totems of these creatures, to help them contact the ancestor spirits.

■ **Many tribes believed** that they would be punished by the animal spirits of their ancestors if they hunted or fished for more food than they needed.

■ **Four sky spirits** were important to the Pawnee – the north star was their creator, the morning star became their protector, the south star led the enemy forces of the underworld, and the evening star brought darkness to the world.

■ **Central tribes believed** that Sedna was the old woman of the sea. She controlled sea creatures and caused storms.

■ **Stories of the Algonquian tribe** say that the goodness of nature came from the god Gluskap. All hostile, poisonous natural things are the work of his brother, Malsum.

■ **South Eastern tribes**, including the Cherokee, built mounds of earth in the shape of sacred animal spirits. Tribal ceremonies were held around these sacred sites.

■ **The Arikara people of the plains** believed that the corn mother taught them agriculture. To keep the peace and have good weather, they made offerings of smoke to the sky spirit.

■ **Shamans were holy men** who knew how to contact spirits. They sometimes used herbs and chanting to sink into a trance, allowing a spirit to enter them and speak.

▶ Native Americans carved pictures of their ancestor spirits into whole tree trunks, known as totem poles. The family spirit animal was usually represented, such as an eagle. Each pole tells the history of a particular family, celebrating brave heroes.

■ **In the late 19th century** many Native American tribes performed ghost dances to ask the spirits of their animal ancestors to drive European settlers from their lands.

■ **According to the Iroquois tribes**, spirits were ruled over by a guardian called the Great Manitou.

Persian deities

■ **The earliest Persians** worshipped nature deities such as Tishtrya, the god of fertility, and Anahita, the goddess of the lakes and oceans.

■ **Three famous priests** of the nature god cult were the Magi – the three wise men or kings who visited baby Jesus.

■ **In ancient times**, the god of victory, Verethragna, was worshipped widely through the Persian empire by soldiers. Like the Hindu god Vishnu, he was born ten times on earth to fight demons. He took different animal and human forms.

■ **The human heroes** of Persian myths and legends were also worshipped as godlike rulers. The hero Faridun battled an evil monster and imprisoned him at the ends of the earth.

▼ *Ruins of the ancient Persian city of Persepolis, such as the great audience hall, are still standing in modern Iran. Mythical creatures of bull-headed men guarded the Gate of All Nations, warding off evil.*

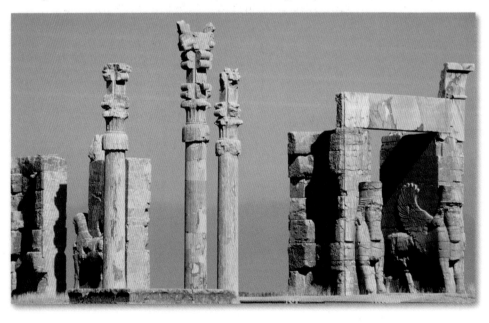

▶ *One Persian myth says that the god Mithras brought fertility to the world. He killed a bull that contained all the strength of the earth, and sprinkled its blood over the land.*

■ **In the first and second century**, the god of light, Mithras, became an important deity. A warrior hero, he protected creation by killing the forces of evil.

■ **From the 6th century**, the beliefs of a prophet called Zoroaster spread through Persia. The religion became known as Zoroastrianism, and the ancient gods became saints called Yazatas.

■ **The chief god in Zoroastrianism**, Ahura Mazda, was a great Persian god. He fought against the evil of the god Ahriman.

■ **According to Persian belief**, Ahura Mazda was Zoroaster's father, borne to him and his wife as a gift from god.

■ **According to Zoroaster**, creation is protected by seven spirit guardians known as Amesha Spentas.

■ **Zoroastrians believe** that everyone is looked after by guardian spirits, or Fravashi. These spirits represent the goodness in people and help those who ask.

Hindu deities

▲ Hindu temples are ornately decorated with statues and carvings of the gods.

■ **Hindus believe** that one day in the life of the supreme spirit, Brahman, is equivalent to 4320 million years on earth.

■ **In Hindu belief**, there is a correct way for everyone to behave, according to their role in society. Myths say that the god Vishnu established this code of good behaviour, known as *dharma*.

■ **The wife of the mighty destroyer god**, Shiva, is an important goddess. She has three forms – the gentle Parvati, the brave demon-fighter Durga, and the bloodthirsty Kali.

■ **Ganesha is the Hindu god** of wisdom. There are many myths to explain why he has an elephant's head. One states that in anger Shiva decapitated Ganesha and had to replace his head with the nearest living thing – an elephant.

■ **Surya is the Hindu god of the sun** and sky. He rides a golden chariot pulled by seven horses.

▼ *The magnificent Hindu temple of Angkor Wat in Cambodia was built to represent Mount Meru, the home of the Hindu gods and goddesses.*

■ **Hindus believe** that gods and goddesses are actually present in their shrines and temples. The picture or statue that represents the god or goddess living there is known as a *murti*.

■ **When Hindus worship** at a shrine or temple, they leave the god or goddess a small offering of food or flowers.

■ **In Hindu art**, gods and goddesses are often painted blue – the Hindu colour of holiness.

■ **Hindu gods and goddesses** are often pictured with several heads or arms, to show their special characteristics. For instance, Vishnu has four arms, two holding objects to show his holiness, and two holding weapons to represent his power.

■ **In 1995**, thousands of people in India reported that statues of Hindu gods were drinking milk. Some people believed this was a miracle. Others said that the statues were made of porous stone that soaked up the liquid.

Celtic religion

■ **Centuries before Christianity**, the Celtic peoples of Great Britain, Ireland and Northern France were led in worship of their gods by priests called Druids.

■ **The name Druid** comes from the Celtic word, *druidh*, which is connected with the Greek word for oak, *drus*. The oak tree was a sacred symbol and Druids held their ceremonies in oak groves.

■ **Celts in different places** called their gods different names and worshipped them in different forms. Danaan is the mother goddess of the Tuatha De Danaan – she is also known as Dana, Danu and Donu.

▼ *Around 2000 BC early Celts built a circle of enormous stones on Salisbury Plain in England. Some historians think it may have been used for worshipping the sun. It is known today as Stonehenge.*

▶ *The leafy face of the nature god, known today simply as the Green Man, is found carved into old buildings across Europe.*

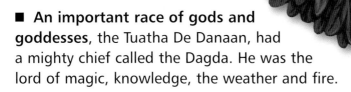

■ **Many myths tell of a horned god** who leads a terrifying wild hunt across the sky. He came to be known as Herne the Hunter.

■ **An important race of gods and goddesses**, the Tuatha De Danaan, had a mighty chief called the Dagda. He was the lord of magic, knowledge, the weather and fire.

■ **Another great leader** of the Tuatha De Danaan was the warrior god Nuada. He had a magic sword that conquered all his enemies.

■ **The hero Lugh** was master of all skills – including magic. After many mighty deeds, he became immortal.

■ **Three important goddesses** are concerned with battle and death – the cruel Morrigan, Macha the goddess of Ulster, and Badb, who sometimes took the form of a raven.

■ **A Celtic god** known today as the Green Man was carved into early Christian churches across the British Isles and Europe. He represented the power of nature, which died and was reborn each year.

■ **In England**, traditional Morris dances re-enact Celtic springtime celebrations. Morris men leap into the air as a symbol of life triumphing over death.

Chinese divinities

■ **For thousands of years**, the Chinese have worshipped the spirits of dead ancestors, believing that they can help the living.

■ **The first emperors in China** ruled over warrior tribes and belonged to a family called the Shang dynasty (c. 1500–1050 BC). They were believed to be gods, as were all the following emperors.

■ **According to many myths**, the first Shang emperor is the most powerful of all Chinese gods. He is known as the Jade Emperor.

■ **The Jade Emperor's wife** was a goddess who grew Peaches of Immortality in her palace gardens. They ripened once every 6000 years.

■ **Chinese emperors built magnificent temples** where they made offerings to the gods on behalf on their people – they asked for good harvests, peace and prosperity.

■ **The first Chinese man** to die and find his way to the underworld became the chief god of the dead, Yen-Lo Wang.

■ **The Chinese believe** that their homes are guarded by special spirits. Tsao Chun is the god of the kitchen. He reports on each family to heaven.

◀ *Laozi taught that a great power, Dao, guides the universe. Legend has it that while travelling on an ox one day, he stopped at a border post to write down his teachings, then was never seen again.*

▲ *A huge palace in Beijing, the Forbidden City, has guardian lions standing at the entrances. The male lion holds a globe under his paw – he protects the outside of the palace. Under the female lion's paw is a cub – she protects the interior.*

■ **As in other civilizations**, throughout the centuries many real Chinese heroes have been turned into legends. The heroes were often made into gods thousands of years after their deaths.

■ **Kuan Ti lived** in the 3rd century AD and became one of China's finest warriors. He became a war god, defending China from enemies.

■ **Wen Chang** was an outstanding student from the 3rd century AD. He was made the god of literature.

Sacrifices for the gods

■ **The Maya used to play** a ball game similar to football. Historians think that at the end of the match, one side was sacrificed to the gods – but they do not know whether it was the winners or the losers.

■ **The first wife of the Hindu god Shiva** was Sati. Sati's father tried to disgrace Shiva, and so Sati threw herself onto a sacred fire as a sacrifice.

■ **The chief Norse god**, Odin, demanded that warriors did not just give themselves up to death fearlessly, but that they actually welcomed death, in his honour.

■ **The ancient Hindu fire god**, Agni, had seven tongues to lick up sacrifices of butter burnt on a sacred fire.

■ **A Bible story** tells how God asked Abraham to offer him his only son, Isaac, as a sacrifice. God stopped Abraham just in time, once he had tested his obedience.

■ **A sacred fire** to the Roman goddess, Vesta, was tended by specially chosen girls called the Vestal Virgins. They had to sacrifice ever getting married.

■ **In Native American tribes**, dancers who wore masks to ward off evil spirits often made offerings of food and 'corn animals' to the good spirits in nature.

▶ *In ancient China, offerings of food and drink were made to ancestor spirits in bronze containers. The vessels were decorated with faces of fierce monsters called* taotie *to ward off evil.*

- **Thousands of people** were sacrificed at a time to the Aztec sun god Huitzilopochtli, who demanded plentiful offerings of human hearts.

- **The Romans often offered** the deaths of gladiators to honour a particular god or goddess.

- **Druid priests** sometimes made sacrifices to the Celtic gods by hanging up criminals or prisoners of war in big wicker cages and burning them alive.

▶ *At Roman gladiatorial games, the winner stood before the emperor with the defeated. The emperor could then dedicate the death to their chosen god or goddess.*

Abraham and Isaac

A Bible story

Thousands of years ago, in the hot, dusty lands around the Red Sea, there lived a devout old couple called Abraham and Sarah. They had longed for children for many years, and had prayed to God countless times to help them – but God had not answered them. Now, they were in the twilight of their lives, but at last the Lord saw fit to respond to their desperate pleas and Sarah gave birth to a baby boy. He was the delight of the couple's eyes and they named him Isaac. Isaac grew up to be a lively, strong child – everything Abraham and Sarah had hoped for. It was their greatest joy to watch Isaac do his homework, run errands, and play in the fields with the other children. Like all proud parents, they dreamed of what he might be in the future … the wife he would choose … the grandchildren he would give them. Their happiness was complete – until one day, Abraham heard God calling him.

"Abraham! Take your only son, Isaac and journey for three days to the south. Go to a mountain that I will show you. There, I want you to offer him to me as a sacrifice."

Abraham was truly horrified. How could God be asking him to kill his own son? The Lord knew how long he and Sarah had been desperate for children, and how precious Isaac was. Abraham's blood ran cold. He would not, could not, refuse the Lord anything. But his only beloved son, the most precious, irreplaceable thing to Abraham. How terrible was the request!

All day long, Abraham sat alone under a broad tree, and refused to come indoors. He could not rest, he could not eat, he could not drink. As evening fell, Abraham fell to his knees in the dust and begged God to change his mind, but the Lord remained silent. "Then give me the strength to carry out this dreadful deed," Abraham prayed, "for I will surely need you to guide my hand if I am to do what you ask." As he staggered indoors, he would not look at either his anxious wife or son. What could he say to Sarah? How could he tell Isaac?

In the end, Abraham mentioned nothing to his family of God's request. The next morning, he rose early and prepared for the journey. Then he took his son and two servants to cut firewood, which they loaded onto a donkey. Abraham looked at the animal's burden and thought that the awful secret he carried within him was far heavier.

Abraham could not watch as Isaac kissed his mother goodbye. And so they set off, with Abraham hanging his head in misery.

"Where are we going, Father?" enquired Isaac, his eyes wide with excitement and wonder.

"Never you mind, son," murmured Abraham, his hands trembling. "All in good time."

Abraham hardly spoke as they plodded along, with the sun beating down on their faces. During the night, he lay awake, staring up at the stars through the material of his tent. At the end of the third day, he knew with dread in his soul that they had reached God's chosen place. He told the servants to wait with the donkey. "Isaac and I are going to make an offering to God," he stated, and then Abraham and Isaac began to climb the steep hillside.

After a while, Isaac grew a little puzzled. "Father, I'm carrying the wood, you have a knife and some flint to start a fire, but where is the lamb we're going to offer?"

Abraham tried hard to keep his voice steady. "My son," he replied with great anguish. "God will provide himself with a lamb."

Side by side, the two eventually reached the spot for the sacrifice. Gathering stones, they built an altar, and Abraham

arranged the firewood. The time had come.
Abraham began to bind his son.

"What are you doing father?" Isaac screamed, struggling to
break free from his bonds as he realized what was about to
happen. "Stop it! Please stop it!"

Abraham tried not to look at Isaac's face as he lifted him onto
the sacrificial pile. With tears streaming down his aged cheeks,
his shoulders heaved with sobs, and his heart felt as if it would
burst into pieces within his chest.

Slowly, Abraham reached for his knife. Overcome by grief, he
steeled himself to obey God. He raised the blade up over his son.

All at once he heard someone calling his name.

"Abraham! Abraham!"

Abraham stopped still. Slowly, he lowered the knife and listened. Then he fell to his knees. It was the voice of the angel of the Lord.

"Here I am," Abraham moaned.

"Abraham!" called the angel of the Lord. "Do not harm the boy! Since you would have given God your only son, he knows now that you are true to him."

Abraham could hardly believe his ears. Slowly, he raised his eyes to look at the trembling, moaning boy tied to the altar. His son had been spared. He fell upon his only child, covering his face with kisses, begging his forgiveness and hastening to untie his bonds.

Suddenly something caught his attention in a thicket nearby. It was a ram, snared in the brambles and struggling to break free. Still weeping with joy, Abraham lifted Isaac down from the firewood. He took the animal and offered it in Isaac's place, giving great thanks to God. And the angel of the Lord called to Abraham for a second time from heaven.

"Abraham, the Lord says that because you have obeyed him, both you and your son shall be blessed. You will have as many descendants as there are stars in the sky, as many descendants as there are grains of sand on the seashore, and they shall become a great people."

With that Abraham and Isaac descended from the mountain, and along with the servants, they began their journey home. Abraham was not only thankful for his precious son, who skipped along the path happily, but also for God's true faith in him. He smiled, content and happy with his life once more.

Gifts from the gods

■ **Greek mythology** tells that when Perseus went to kill the Gorgon, the gods gave him a helmet of invisibility, winged sandals, and a highly polished bronze shield – with a clue to use it as a mirror.

■ **According to Egyptian myth**, the god Osiris taught people the skill of farming and gave them laws and religious rites.

■ **Legend has it that the French peasant girl** Joan of Arc heard God telling her to go into an ancient church and dig behind the altar. She found a great sword that had been used in holy wars called the Crusades.

■ **A Greek myth** says that King Midas asked the gods for 'the golden touch' – anything he touched was turned into gold. He soon regretted the gift when he tried to eat and drink.

■ **The Japanese sun goddess**, Amaterasu, was once found hiding in a cave by the other gods. They enticed her to come out with the gift of the first ever mirror.

■ **Inuit myths** tell how it was the raven who brought many gifts to humans, including daylight.

■ **In Greek myth**, the goddess Thetis knew her hero son, Achilles, would die in the Trojan War. She tried to protect him with armour made by the gods' blacksmith, Hephaestus.

■ **A Christian story** says that when Jesus was on his way to die on the cross, a woman called Veronica wiped his bleeding face. The imprint of Jesus' features was left on her handkerchief.

■ **The *Ramayana* tells** how the great god, Indra, gave the monkey hero, Hanuman, the power to choose his own death, as a gift for helping Prince Rama.

■ **The Greek goddess Athene gave the hero** Bellerophon a golden bridle with which he could catch the magical winged horse, Pegasus.

▼ *In ancient Greek mythology, the Corinthian prince, Bellerophon, tamed the winged stallion, Pegasus, and they had many courageous adventures together. After Bellerophon was killed, Pegasus carried thunderbolts for the chief god Zeus.*

Making mischief

■ **In Native American myths**, the trickster god Coyote uses his cunning to help the human race, for example, by getting rid of giants.

■ **The Polynesian god Maui** is one of the greatest troublemakers of all. He also sometimes uses his tricks to help humans – he once slowed the sun down as it moved across the sky to give humans more daylight.

■ **Kobolds were a type of earth spirit** or dwarf said to live in German silver mines. They enjoyed causing trouble for human miners, such as explosions and rockfalls.

■ **The Aborigines of Arnhem Land** in the Northern Territory of Australia believe in rock spirits called Mimi. The Mimi can be kind and helpful to humans, but if strangers disturb them, they cause severe illnesses as punishment.

■ **Stories from the Caribbean** tell of a half-man, half-spider character called Anansi. He loves to create havoc for his archenemy, Tiger.

◄ *Mischievous and cruel, trolls feature in many Scandinavian myths. They often live deep inside hills and mountains, only emerging to cause trouble to humans.*

▶ *Leprechauns are known for their mischief. Legend has it that they are cobblers by trade, who have secret hoards of hidden gold.*

■ **Japanese mythology** is filled with ghost stories. The spirits of the dead often cause trouble for those who hurt them while they were alive.

■ **Some people believe** that the power of the great Celtic god Lugh dwindled away over the centuries until he became a mischievous sprite called a 'lugh-chromain' or leprechaun.

■ **In Eastern European myth**, a kikimora is a female house spirit. If the household is kept dirty and untidy, the kikimora will whine, whistle and tickle the children at night.

■ **Pilots and engineers used to blame** sprites called Gremlins for anything that went wrong with their aircraft.

■ **Loki was a famous trickster** in Norse mythology who enjoyed stirring up trouble between the gods and the giants.

Trickery

■ **Native American Algonquian myth** says that the god Gluskap thought that there was no one in the universe who would disobey him. A woman defeated his boast by bringing him her baby, which of course would not listen to a word he said.

■ **The Egyptian goddess Isis** created a poisonous snake to bite the sun god, Ra. Isis would only cure him if he told her his secret name.

▶ *In American folklore, Brer Rabbit is a great trickster. In one tale Brer Fox tries to catch him using sticky tar, but Brer Rabbit uses his cunning to escape.*

■ **In Norse mythology**, prophecies said that a mighty wolf called Fenris would kill the chief god, Odin. The gods found a way to trick Fenris into being tied up with a ribbon made of strong magic.

■ **The Tupinamba people** of South America once thought that a great shaman, Maira-Monan, was growing too powerful. They tricked him into walking into a fire of powerful magic, which killed him.

■ **Osiris, the great god of Egypt**, was secretly murdered in a trick by his jealous brother, Seth. Under false pretences Seth coaxed Osiris into a coffin, then he slammed the lid shut so Osiris suffocated.

■ **According to Greek myth**, the Titan Prometheus tricked the chief god Zeus into accepting animal bones and fat from humans as sacrifices. Ever since, humans have been allowed to keep the meat for themselves.

■ **A Native American myth** tells how the god Coyote tried to smoke a rabbit out of his burrow. The rabbit cleverly hurled the fire back at him.

■ **In Chinese myth**, the Jade Emperor once gave Monkey the job of keeper of the heavenly horse. This sounded like an important honour, but in fact, Monkey was just a stable boy!

■ **Myths from the South Pacific islands** tell of the god Maui who tried to trick the goddess Hina into granting immortality to the world. The furious Hina crushed Maui to death.

■ **Norse myth says** that the blind god Hodur was tricked into killing his twin brother Baldur, who was loved by all creation. This was the beginning of the end for the warrior gods.

The Murder of Osiris

An ancient Egyptian myth

The creator, the sun god Ra, ruled the heavens and gave the
god, Osiris, the task of looking after the world. Osiris made
his home in Ra's favourite country, Egypt. There, he ruled
as king with his wife, the mighty goddess Isis, as his queen.

Wise and fair, Osiris cared deeply for his people and, in return,
his people loved him. Under his guidance, the Egyptians learnt how
to farm the land and tend the animals. The great god brought law
and order to the country. Most importantly, he taught everyone
how to worship the other gods properly. Before long, Egypt became
a prosperous place where all the people lived happily.

Everyone loved Osiris – except, that is, for his youngest brother,
the god Seth. Seth was jealous of Osiris and exceedingly bitter that
Ra had chosen Osiris to be king of Egypt instead of him.

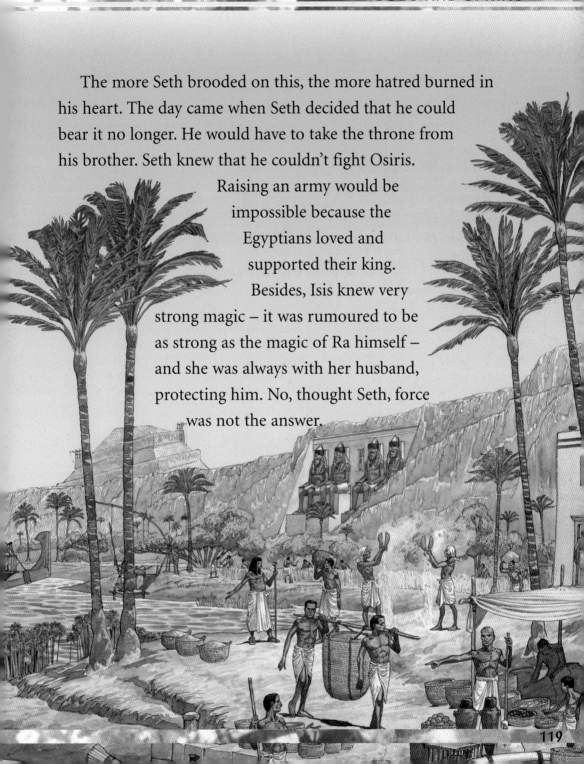

The more Seth brooded on this, the more hatred burned in his heart. The day came when Seth decided that he could bear it no longer. He would have to take the throne from his brother. Seth knew that he couldn't fight Osiris. Raising an army would be impossible because the Egyptians loved and supported their king. Besides, Isis knew very strong magic – it was rumoured to be as strong as the magic of Ra himself – and she was always with her husband, protecting him. No, thought Seth, force was not the answer.

He would have to be much more cunning than that.

Seth waited until Osiris went away, then he seized the opportunity to bribe the royal craftsmen and courtiers into helping him. He paid them handsomely, and they listened carefully to his plan …

Months later, when Osiris returned from his travels, there were great celebrations throughout Egypt. The people feasted in their homes, and sang and danced in the streets. A mighty banquet was held at the palace – and of course, Seth was one of the guests.

Usually at royal parties, Seth sat in a corner and glowered. But today was different. Today his heart was filled with a gleeful secret, and Seth couldn't stop himself from smiling and laughing along with all the other guests. Admiring the beautiful decorations of garlands, banners and scented candles, he helped himself to platefuls of the tasty food and drank goblet after goblet of wine. When the musicians began playing, he clapped along, and roared with delight at the acrobats and jugglers. Finally, when everyone had eaten, Seth stood up and bellowed for silence.

"Welcome home, brother Osiris!" he announced, with a grand flourish. "In honour of your return, I have arranged some very special fun for us all."

Seth clapped his hands, and beckoned his group of courtiers to enter the banqueting hall. Everyone turned and watched as the men came in, carrying in a long, narrow chest, made of gold and decorated with precious gems in intricate designs. The banquet guests all gasped in admiration of the beautiful object.

"Brother, this wonderful chest, shining like the rays of Ra himself, has been made by your own royal craftsmen," Seth explained – not mentioning that he had bribed them to make it in a very special way. "It is the prize in a new game – one that is very easy to play. Each of us will take turns to lie inside it, and whoever fits exactly – head touching one end and feet the other, with the sides snug around them – wins the chest!"

The banquet guests were thrilled and hurried to queue up to take their turn in the game. One by one, they all lay down in the chest, and one by one, they were all disappointed. They were either too tall or too short, too big or too small. At last, only Osiris himself was left.

"Come, brother!" Seth encouraged. "Let us see if fortune is smiling upon you this evening."

Gathering his robes around him, Osiris stepped carefully into the chest. Then the courtiers helped him to lie down. It was a tight squeeze, but if he held his breath, he fitted exactly inside!

The watching guests all went wild with delight.

"We have a winner!" Seth cheered. "Congratulations brother!"

Motioning for the musicians to strike up and play, he seized Isis and swept her off in a joyous dance. Everyone joined in, laughing with pleasure – leaving Osiris lying in the chest, trapped.

Soon only the courtiers remained around the chest – everyone else was whirling around the dance floor, enjoying themselves, the game quite forgotten. Quick as a flash, without anyone noticing, the courtiers slammed the lid shut. Then they picked the chest up and hurried out of the banqueting hall.

Leaving the revellers dancing and singing, the courtiers took the chest to the river Nile and threw it into the deeps – just as Seth had paid them to. The golden coffin sank down deeper and deeper into the dark waters … where Osiris eventually suffocated to death.

Meanwhile, Isis searched high and low for Osiris, but he did not reappear that night, nor the night after, nor any of the nights after that. As time passed, Egypt mourned, but it eventually became clear that there was no option but to declare Seth the new king. However, while Seth was triumphant, Isis was heartbroken. She swore never to rest until she found out what had happened to her beloved husband.

The Trojan War

■ **Iliad is an epic poem** that tells of events at the end of a ten-year war between the ancient Greeks and the Trojans. It is the earliest written work from ancient Greece.

■ **Goddesses and gods play a major role** in *Iliad*. They support different sides, giving their human favourites advice and help.

■ **The Trojan War** began when the Trojan Prince, Paris, kidnapped Queen Helen of Sparta. Her father asked the Greeks to help win her back.

■ **When *Iliad*** was composed, no written records about the Trojan War existed. The story comes from information passed down by word of mouth for hundreds of years.

■ **Archaeologists, including Heinrich Schliemann, have discovered** remains of **the city of Troy**, which burned in 1184 BC. The historic site is actually situated in Anatolia, northwest Turkey.

■ **The principal characters** in *Iliad* are the courageous noblemen of both sides. They aim to win fame by fighting honourably and dying a glorious warrior's death.

◄ *This painting on an ancient Greek vase shows the warrior Achilles. He was protected by divine armour – except for a small spot on his heel, which is where he finally received his death wound.*

▶ German archaeologist Heinrich Schliemann found the Mask of Agamemnon at Mycenae in 1876. Archaeologists now believe that the death mask actually dates 300 years before the life of Agamemnon.

■ **The Greek commander Agamemnon sailed** the Greek army to Troy. He led the army in battle, fighting until he was badly wounded.

■ **The greatest Greek warrior** is Achilles. When he argues with the Greek commander, Agamemnon, and withdraws from battle, the Greek army suffers terribly.

■ **The greatest Trojan warrior** is Paris' brother, Hector. He is eventually killed by Achilles.

■ **The Greeks eventually won** the Trojan War. The hero Odysseus had the idea of building a huge wooden horse, inside which many Greek warriors hid. The Greeks left it outside the gates of Troy and the Trojans took it inside the city, thinking it was a gift. At night, the Greek warriors scrambled out and destroyed the city.

125

The Trojan Horse

From the epic poem *Iliad*

When Prince Paris of Troy stole away the beautiful Helen, wife of King Menelaus of Greece, the outraged Greeks were determined to win her back. The finest warriors in the swiftest ships sailed in a mighty fleet to the shores of their enemy. Eventually hundreds of warriors swarmed up the beaches, laying siege to the immense, high-walled city of Troy.

The Trojan princes often descended from their lofty towers to pit their strength against the Greeks on the broad plain outside the steadfast gates. Among the armies of both sides were the greatest heroes the world has ever seen. At their hands, the battlefield ran red with rivers of blood by day, and burned with smoking funeral pyres by night.

After ten long years, even the Trojan princes Paris and Hector, and the Greek warrior of warriors Achilles, were ranked among the slain. Yet the Greeks were still no closer to breaching the towering stone stronghold. Battle-weary, disheartened and homesick, the great army was out of ideas – until the great king Odysseus hit upon a daring new plan. If they could not win the city of Troy by force, they might instead win it by cunning.

Odysseus ordered soldiers to a nearby forest on Mount Ida to cut down trees and chop them into planks. Then the famous carpenter, Epeius, set to work with the wood. After three days, he had crafted an enormous wooden horse that was stunning to behold. It was so magnificent that no one guessed it was in fact hollow. A hidden trapdoor led up into the empty body.

At dawn the following day, the sentries positioned high on the battlements of Troy could not believe their eyes. Every morning for the past ten years, they had been greeted by the sight of the Greek camp spreading along the shore, their banners fluttering in the breeze, their armour glinting in the sunlight, their ships filling the water as far as the eye could see. But this morning, the beach was empty! Or nearly – among the smoking heaps of burning huts was the incredible sight of the giant wooden horse, standing still and silent on the golden sands. The sentries sounded the alarm at once.

When old King Priam of Troy surveyed the scene for himself, he was nervous that the Greeks might have set an ambush. A group of scouts marched down to the seashore to investigate – but they found only one Greek soldier hiding among the rocks. Terrified, he begged the Trojans to spare his life, telling them that the Greeks had sailed for home, leaving the horse as a gift and himself as a sacrifice to the gods, to ask for a safe voyage.

Joy rushed into the hearts of the Trojans and after endless battles, they had cause to celebrate. Throwing open the gates of the city, the men, women and children ran down to the sea for the first time in ten years. Singing and dancing, they attached ropes to the wooden horse and laid rollers in front of it. By nightfall, they had heaved it into the heart of Troy. Then the elated citizens ate, drank and danced until the early hours, when everyone fell asleep – even the sentries.

Alas for Troy! Fortune was not smiling on the city after all. The Greek warrior had courageously volunteered to weave a web of lies. As soon as the Trojans had started feasting, the entire Greek fleet had sailed back to their beaches from a nearby cove. Now, in the city, with the Trojans soundly snoring, the trapdoor in the wooden horse slid open. Odysseus and a band of the finest Greek warriors descended from inside. Some of the warriors headed straight for Helen's chamber, while the others opened the gates of Troy, unleashing hell on the great city.

The Trojans had no chance and were slaughtered in their beds. In triumph, the victorious Greeks led Helen down to their ships and set their torches to the great city. Finally, as the sun rose, the Greeks set off on their long journey home, leaving Troy to burn.

Beowulf

- **The epic poem** *Beowulf* was written in the Anglo-Saxon language by an unknown English person around AD 700–750.

- **The legend focuses** on the adventures of a Viking hero, Beowulf, and takes place in the south of Sweden and Denmark.

- **Christianity was introduced** to England around AD 600. The poem blends traditional elements of Norse myth, such as warrior culture and fate, with belief in a Christian god.

- **Beowulf risks his life** to help other people by battling three terrifying monsters – Grendel, Grendel's mother, and a dragon.

- **The monster Grendel** is said to bear 'the mark of Cain'. This is a reference to the Bible story in which Adam's son Cain killed his brother Abel. Sent away, Cain feared he would be killed. God placed a curse on him, so no one would harm him.

- **Beowulf is fatally wounded** when all his chosen warriors desert him through fear – except for his courageous nephew Wiglaf.

- **At the end of the poem**, the dead Beowulf is laid to rest in a huge burial mound.

- **The oldest existing manuscript** of *Beowulf* was made from an original by monks in about AD 1000. Many other older copies were destroyed when King Henry VIII ordered monasteries and their libraries to be closed down in the late 1530s.

- **The only remaining copy** of the epic is kept in a controlled environment behind glass in the British Museum in London, England.

- **The modern-day film** *The Thirteenth Knight* starring Antonio Banderas is based on the Beowulf legend.

▼ Beowulf descends to the depths of a murky lake to fight the monster Grendel's ferocious mother after she attacks his warriors.

Kotan Utunnai

■ **The epic poem** *Kotan Utunnai* belongs to a race of people from the Stone Age called the Ainu.

■ **The Ainu lived** on remote Japanese islands, untouched by the outside world for hundreds of years, until other Japanese people made contact in around AD 1670.

■ **Living simply by hunting and gathering, the Ainu** had no agricultural systems, no metalworking skills and no system of writing.

■ **An English missionary** first wrote down *Kotan Utunnai* in the 1880s.

■ *Kotan Utunnai* **is one of several Ainu epic poems** that focus on wars with a people called the Okhotsk from the 10th–16th centuries.

■ **The hero of** *Kotan Utunnai* puts family loyalty above his own desires. This means he has to seek revenge for the murder of his parents.

■ **With godlike qualities**, the hero of *Kotan Utunnai* is so godlike that even the gods themselves sometimes find it hard to believe he is human.

■ **In the myth**, the world of humans is strangely mixed up with the magical world of gods, spirits and demons. From time to time humans hear the sound of gods fighting like a low rumbling across the land.

■ **Unlike many other epics**, there are several powerful female characters in *Kotan Utunnai*. Women have great fighting skills and are considered equal to men.

▲ *The earliest people in Japan, the Ainu, wore Attush coats. The patterns around all the openings of the coat were designed to stop evil spirits from entering.*

■ **The poem demonstrates** the Ainu belief that when you die, if you have led a good life, you will be reborn. However, if you were a wrongdoer, you will remain dead.

Kotan Utunnai

A Japanese myth

I was raised by a young woman I called my older sister – although she was not my sister by blood. My sister's people were the people of the sea, enemies of my people – the people of the land. My sister told me that my father and mother were great warriors, who died bravely together in battle when I was only a baby. The woman I now call my sister took pity on me and from then on, took care of me and gave me all the love I could ever need – even though she was of the enemy. So, I was brought up here in this lonely place, far away from humans and their dangers.

When I was little, I sometimes heard a rumbling sound far off. My sister said this was the sound of her people's gods fighting. When I grew older, I sometimes heard a rumbling sound overhead, upon the roof of our grass hut. Somehow I knew that this was made by the spirits of my own people. When I told my sister, she revealed that I had an older brother who had also survived, and who had declared war on the people of the sea, to avenge the death of my parents. I knew I had to find him.

I asked my older sister for my father's clothes, which she had saved carefully. Soon I stood proudly in my father's war robes, with his helmet on my head, and his sword thrust into his belt at my waist. Feeling my father's spirit rush into my body, I was suddenly whisked with my sister up through the smoke hole of our hut and we were carried away on the wind.

Up through the skies we were blown in a blur, and finally dropped gently on the shores of a sandy beach, not far from a range of towering mountains. With great leaps and bounds, my sister and I set off over several forests, which we realized were made of strange metal trees. Finally, we came to a great bonfire, surrounded by six men wearing stone armour, six men wearing metal armour, twelve women, and a monstrous, revoltingly ugly demon.

To my horror, tied to the top of one of the metal trees was a terribly wounded man. Although I had never laid eyes on him before, I knew at once that he was my older brother, Kamui-otopush.

"Do you admire our prisoner?" growled the demon. "We are taking him as a sacrifice to our leader and ruler, Shipish-un-kur!"

Outraged, I instantly drew my sword to do battle for his life. With one stroke, I killed three of the stone warriors and their wives, and with a second stroke, I killed three of the metal warriors and their wives. Meanwhile, my sister sprang to the top of the tree and freed Kamui-otopush. Within minutes, she had spirited him away to safety, and returned to my side.

Together, my sister and I took on the hideous demon and the remaining men and women. Our sword blades flashed as we slashed and sliced through the air in the direction of the mountains. I prayed to the gods for help, and felt my father's fighting spirit flood through me afresh. One by one, I killed them all – even the terrible demon. One by one, their spirits left their bodies and flew rumbling away into the west.

Perplexed, my sister and I felt the need to face Shipish-un-kur and punish him for wanting Kamui-otopush killed.

Following our instincts, we journeyed for half a day before we finally came to Shipish-un-kur's house. Peering in cautiously at the window, we saw that Shipish-un-kur was only a young man, with scarcely any hairs on his chin. Sitting next to him was the most beautiful young woman I had ever seen – his younger sister, Shipish-un-mat. Without further hesitation, I left my sister and flew up onto the roof of their house, stomping about to make as much noise as possible. With one swift movement, I dropped down the chimney and seized Shipish-un-kur. "You would have taken my older brother as a trophy!" I roared. "Instead, you will face my sword. Now fight me – or die like a coward!"

Letting go of Shipish-un-kur, I grabbed his sister, thinking to use her as a shield. But Shipish-un-kur was not deterred, and simply stabbed her repeatedly. This filled Shipish-un-mat with such fury that she turned against her brother and began to fight

on my side. Up, down and around we flew inside the house, springing off the rafters, smashing into the walls and bouncing off the floor, entangled and entwined in combat. Hearing all the noise we were creating, an army of Shipish-un-kur's finest warriors hurtled in to defend him. Fortunately, I was not alone and in a rush of air, Kamui-otopush was suddenly fighting at my side.

Even though I fought with my father's sword, I could not match my brother's skill. Kamui-otopush had the strength of one hundred men, and as he swiped his sword gracefully through the air, the evil warriors fell without a chance.

All at once, Shipish-un-mat screamed out a prophecy, "Your older sister has travelled to a far-distant land. She is fighting demons and is sorely wounded. She is in dire need of your help!"

"Go!" cried Kamui-otopush. "I will finish off these vermin and then I will join you."

Shipish-un-mat and I flew up into the heavens. My sister's spirit led me to her, and to my dismay I saw that Shipish-un-mat's words were true. Lifting my sister's crumpled body to the heavens, I begged the gods to restore her to health. To my eternal joy, they answered my prayer and she was well again.

And so my sister married the hero Kamui-otopush. I married the beautiful Shipish-un-mat. And from then on, the people of the sea and the people of the land have lived together in peace and harmony.

Finn McCool

■ **The legend of Finn McCool** may be based on a warrior hero who lived in Ireland in the 3rd century AD.

■ **As a boy, Finn's name** was Demna. His teacher, Finn the Poet, gave him the name Finn, meaning fair haired.

■ **Finn was raised** in secret by a druidess and a wise woman, who taught him godlike powers of strength and speed.

■ **Finn was very wise** and just. This is because he once ate a magical fish called the Salmon of Knowledge.

▲ *Legend says that the hero Finn McCool created the rock formation called the Giants' Causeway in Northern Ireland. In fact, it was formed when lava from a volcano cooled and set.*

▶ *This Celtic cross shows Finn McCool with his thumb in his mouth. He is touching his magical 'tooth of knowledge', which had an extraordinary power, telling him whatever he wanted to know.*

■ **After Finn ate the Salmon of Knowledge**, when he put his finger in his mouth, anything he needed to know became clear.

■ **Finn won the position** of head of the Fianna – an elite group of warriors sworn to defend the High King of Ireland. Under his leadership, the Fianna had many daring, magical adventures.

■ **The Fianna possessed** a magic treasure bag that contained weapons from the gods, objects with healing powers, and fairy gifts.

■ **Finn fell in love** with the goddess, Sava. She bore him a son, Oisin, who became a famous Fianna warrior and a great poet.

■ **Finn once had an argument** with a giant in Scotland. They threw rocks across the sea at one another, creating a rock formation today called the Giants' Causeway.

■ **Legend says that Finn** and the Fianna lived on the Hill of Allen in present-day County Kildare.

The Giant's Wife

An Irish legend

*I*n the days when giants lived in the north of Ireland, Finn McCool was the biggest, strongest, most handsome of them all – or so he thought. With his bare hands, Finn could rip a pine tree out of the ground. He could leap across a river in one bound. He could split a boulder in half with one swish of his axe. Surely he was the greatest giant who ever lived …

Now Finn had heard that there were clans of giants living in Scotland who had competitions throwing tree trunks and carrying boulders. That sounded to him like great fun. So Finn decided to build a road right across the sea, so he could walk across to see these Scottish giants without getting his feet wet. Pulling on his big black workboots, he kissed his wife Oonagh goodbye, and promised, "I'll be back in about a week – ten days, tops." Then he strode off over the hills and forests to the coast.

Finn began to work hard, ripping rocks from the mountains and throwing them into the sea until they piled up above the water and began to form a road. He was only three days into the job when a friend of his arrived at the seashore. "Finn, I don't mean to worry you, to be sure," his friend said, "but there's gossip about a strange giant who's on his way to your house to flatten you. Some say that he's leapt across the sea from Scotland without needing a boat or a bridge. People say that he keeps a thunderbolt in his pocket. I've heard, too, that he has a magic little finger with as much strength in it as ten men put together!"

"Pah!" cried Finn, "I don't believe a word of it!" But secretly, he began to feel a little uneasy.

"One thing's for sure," his friend continued, "the stranger knows that everyone thinks you're the biggest, strongest, most handsome giant in all of Ireland, and he doesn't like it one little bit. He's made up his mind to find you and mince you into pieces!"

"We'll see about that!" bellowed Finn. "I'm going home right now to sit and wait for this pipsqueak of a giant. If he dares to show his face at my front door, I'll stamp on him and squash him like an ant!" Although Finn sounded brave, he was really rather worried.

The minute Finn arrived home, he sat down glumly at the kitchen table and told Oonagh all about the stories of the strange giant.

"If it's true, he'll beat me into mashed potatoes!" Finn moaned.

"You men are always boasting about your muscles, but

sometimes you should use your brains instead," Oonagh laughed.
"Now do as I say and leave everything else to me."

Oonagh quickly found nine round, flat stones and put them on
a plate with a round flat oatcake, which she cleverly marked with a
thumbprint so she could see which one it was. Meanwhile, Finn
built an enormous baby's cradle and put it by the fireside, just as
Oonagh had told him. Just then, Finn and Oonagh felt the ground
begin to shake underneath them and a dark shadow fell across the
house.

"It's him! He's here!" panicked Finn, running to and fro. "What
shall I do?"

"Calm down," urged Oonagh, handing her husband a bonnet
and a nightdress. "Put these on and climb into the cradle!"

Finn was far too scared to argue, and soon he was dressed up
like a baby and lying cuddled up in the crib. Oonagh shoved a
huge bottle of milk into his mouth and went to answer the door.

"WHERE IS FINN MCCOOL?" roared the massive giant. He
was certainly the biggest giant Oonagh had ever seen – and the
ugliest! "WHEN I FIND HIM, I'M GOING TO RIP HIM TO
SHREDS!" the giant bellowed.

"I'm afraid you've missed my husband," Oonagh smiled
sweetly. "He's away at the coast, building a road across the sea to
Scotland. He started this morning and he'll be finished by teatime.
You can come and wait for him if you like."

The massive giant growled something under his breath that may or may not have been a thank you.

Oonagh beckoned him inside. "Well, you'd better come in and have something to eat. You'll need to get your strength up if you're going to fight Finn. I have to say, you look like a dwarf next to my husband!"

In the cradle, Finn's teeth began to chatter. What on earth was his wife annoying the monster giant like that for?

"Have an oatcake," Oonagh offered the stranger politely,

putting one of the round, flat rocks on his plate.

The greedy giant crammed it into his mouth and took a huge bite. "OW!" he roared, spitting broken teeth all over the table.

"Oh dear, didn't you like it?" Oonagh fussed. "To be sure, they're the baby's favourite!" She strode over to the cradle and gave Finn the oatcake with the thumbprint. He munched on it happily.

The strange giant peered into the cradle. "That's Finn McCool's baby?" he asked, surprised. "He's a whopper of a lad, isn't he?"

"Yes," sighed Oonagh, tickling her husband under the chin while Finn cooed and gurgled as best he could. "He's got teeth already, you know. Here, put your finger into his mouth and feel. Go on."

Slowly, nervously, the giant put his little finger inside Finn's mouth.

CRUNCH! Finn bit down as hard as he could – right through the bone!

The giant roared in pain. "If Finn McCool's baby is that strong, I'm not staying to find out what Finn McCool is like!" With that, he was out of the door and away over the hills before Finn could even leap out of the cradle.

Finn McCool never did finish his road across the sea. If you go to Ireland, you can still see it poking out into the water, half-finished. He wanted nothing more than to stay at home and enjoy the rest of his days with his clever wife. So that's exactly what he did!

King Arthur

- **Legends about an extraordinary** British king called Arthur have been popular for over 800 years, yet historians have never been able to prove whether he was a real figure in history.

- **If Arthur did really exist**, he is likely to have lived much earlier than the medieval times of the legends.

- **Many authors have written** Arthurian legends over the centuries, including the French medieval poet Chretien de Troyes, the 15th-century writer Sir Thomas Malory, and the Victorian poet Lord Tennyson.

- **Arthur's father** was said to be King Uther Pendragon. The name means 'dragon's head'.

▼ *Mont-Saint-Michel is a rocky islet off the coast of northwest France, where legend says King Arthur once slew a giant.*

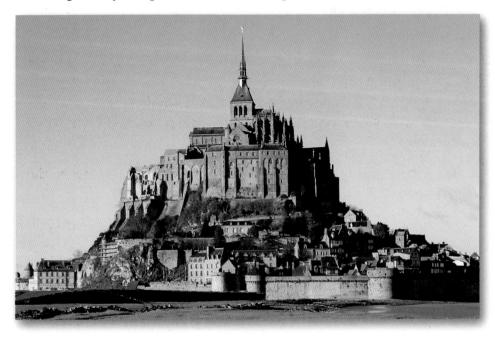

▶ *King Arthur was finally killed by his own son, Mordred. One legend says that his body was buried at the holy site of Glastonbury.*

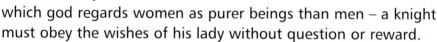

■ **One legend says** that Arthur slew a fearsome giant at Mont-Saint-Michel in France, then conquered the Roman Empire.

■ **Many legends focus** on the knights at Arthur's court and the idea of courtly love, in which god regards women as purer beings than men – a knight must obey the wishes of his lady without question or reward.

■ **Arthur's knights went on** many dangerous quests to test their bravery and honour. The most difficult was a search for the Holy Grail – a goblet that caught Jesus' blood as he died on the cross. The goblet was believed to disappear when anyone who had sinned came near it.

■ **The Round Table** was first mentioned in legends written by the French medieval poet, Robert Wace, in AD 1155.

■ **Arthur is finally killed** by his enemy Mordred – who is actually his son.

■ **Some legends say** that King Arthur was taken to a country of blessed souls called Avalon and will return when Britain falls into greatest danger.

The Sword in the Stone

A Celtic legend

Long, long ago when knights battled fearlessly with dragons and wizards and witches lived in the depths of the forests, every man worth his weight in armour was tested to see if he were brave enough to be knighted king of the Britons …

One cold Christmas morning, the villagers were safely at home in front of their raging fires when something strange happened. In the courtyard of the cathedral, a blacksmith's anvil standing on a huge stone mysteriously appeared. No one knew how it had got there. Even stranger was that the anvil had a sword stuck into it and words were carved right round it saying:

Whoever pulls out this sword is
the rightful king of the Britons.

Many a proud lord stepped up and tried to pull the sword out of the mysterious anvil. But even though they heaved and sweated and grunted, and pulled and pulled and pulled, all of them walked away disappointed. Everyone was dumbfounded. Now almost a week had passed. It was time for the New Year's Eve jousting festival, and still the anvil stood on the stone in the courtyard with the sword sticking out of it, glinting in the winter sunshine.

Every year, bold knights came to the capital city from all over the kingdom to ride against each other in the New Year's Eve jousting festival. It was the ultimate contest in bravery and the knights liked to show off! This particular year Sir Ector's son, Sir Kay, would joust for the very first time. Sir Ector's younger son Arthur was also going along as Sir Kay's squire.

Sir Ector and his sons lived in the furthest corner of the kingdom – so far away from the capital city that news of the strange anvil hadn't even reached them. After three days of hard riding, they at last saw the towering cathedral spire and the bright fluttering flags of the jousting field in the distance.

Suddenly a dreadful thing happened. Sir Kay put his hand down by his side to pat his trusty sword – and there was nothing there.

"My sword!" Sir Kay gasped. "It's gone!"

Arthur turned quite pale with horror. It was a squire's job to make sure that a knight was properly equipped. "We must have left it at the lodging house we stayed at last night," he groaned. "Don't worry Kay. I'll dash back and fetch it." Before anyone could argue, Arthur had wheeled his horse around and was galloping at full speed back down the road. There wasn't a second to lose.

When Arthur arrived back at the lodging house, he hunted high and low, in every nook and cranny. But there was no sign of Sir Kay's sword anywhere. Arthur's heart pounded. "What am I going to do?" he groaned to himself. "My brother won't be able to enter his first New Year's joust after all – and it's all my fault!"

Empty-handed, Arthur raced his horse towards the city once more, wondering how he was going to break the bad news to his brother. He was very nearly at the jousting field when he galloped past the cathedral courtyard and saw the sword sticking out of the anvil on the stone. Arthur reined in his panting horse to take a closer look. How odd, he thought. Who would leave their sword unguarded? Arthur looked all around him. There was no one about – everyone was at the jousting competition. Surely the sword won't be missed if I borrow it for a while, he thought. "I swear I'll bring it back later," Arthur promised out loud to no one in particular.

He dashed over the snow, jumped up onto the stone and grasped the sword. It slid out of the anvil as easily as a needle pulls through cloth. Arthur gazed at the mighty, jewelled blade in his hands. "This is the most magnificent weapon I have ever seen!" Sprinting back to his horse, he leapt into the saddle, and arrived at the jousting field just as the first fanfares were being trumpeted.

Sir Kay was astonished at the superb weapon that his younger brother handed him. He and his father had just heard all about the mysterious anvil from the other knights at the jousting competition, and Kay realized at once where the unique sword must have come from. "See, father!' he cried over the crowds, brandishing the sword over his head. "I must be the new king of the Britons!"

Sir Ector came running at once and gasped at the magnificent weapon in Kay's hands. "Surely it can't be," he murmured, taking it from Kay and examining it in wonderment. "But it must be … I have never in all my years seen a weapon like this." Looking at Kay sternly, he demanded, "How have you come by this?"

Kay's face fell. "Arthur brought it to me," he mumbled.

Sir Ector's face was grave. "Who pulled this out of the stone and gave it to you?" he quizzed Arthur.

"N-n-o one," stammered Arthur, nervously. "I pulled it out of the stone myself. I was going to put it back, honest!"

Sir Ector led Arthur to the cathedral and into the courtyard, ith a huge and excited crowd following hot on their heels. "Put the sword back where you found it, son," he told Arthur.

"All right," shrugged Arthur, wondering why no one had yet accused him of stealing. Surely Sir Ector would soon announce a horrible punishment. Arthur sighed. He climbed onto the stone and thrust the sword back into the anvil. He turned reluctantly back to Sir Ector, ready to be severely reprimanded. But to Arthur's astonishment, Sir Ector didn't utter a word. He just clambered up onto the stone himself and tried to pull the sword out again. After several efforts, huffing and puffing, Sir Ector gave up. He stood back, wiping his brow. "You try, Sir Kay," he instructed his eldest son. Sir Kay heaved at it with all his might. The sword didn't budge an inch. "Now show us how you did it, my boy," said Sir Ector to Arthur, his voice trembling slightly.

Everyone held their breath as Arthur stepped up to the anvil. As he pulled the sword out effortlessly, an almighty cheer erupted. And from that moment on the young boy Arthur, who wasn't even a knight, was crowned king of the Britons.

The Ramayana

- **The Indian epic poem** the *Ramayana* focuses on the battle between the forces of good and evil in the universe.

- **Historians believe** that the poem was largely composed between 200 BC and AD 200.

- **The poet is believed** to be called Valmiki, although hardly anything is known about him.

- **Like the Greek epic**, *Iliad*, the *Ramayana* involves the rescue of a stolen queen. Also, the poem follows a hero on a long and difficult journey, which is similar to the Greek epic, *Odyssey*.

- **Prince Rama's enemy** is the mighty demon Ravana. With 20 arms and ten heads, Ravana can work powerful magic, but he is not immortal.

▲ The hero Rama was a great archer and defeated his enemy Ravana with a poisoned arrow.

■ **The demon Ravana's followers** are known as Rakshasas. They can change shape to disguise themselves, so they do not appear evil. This way, they can tempt good people to do the wrong thing.

■ **The poem demonstrates** that it is important to respect animals. Rama needs the help of the hero Hanuman and his army of monkeys to rescue Sita.

■ **The story says that Rama** and Sita are earthly forms of the great god Vishnu and his wife Lakshmi.

■ **Hindus see the *Ramayana*** as a book of religious teaching because Rama and Sita are models of good behaviour.

■ **The legend ends** when Rama has ruled as king for 10,000 years and is taken up to heaven with his brothers.

▶ *The monkey god Hanuman was the son of the wind and helped Rama in the battle against Ravana.*

The Capture of Sita

From the *Ramayana*

T his tale begins in a time of old, when the evil demon king Ravana terrorized the world with his wicked ways. With ten heads and twenty arms, he was terrifying to behold. He had tricked Brahma, the lord of creation, into giving him special powers of protection. Now no god or demon could harm Ravana, and he was threatening to take over heaven and earth.

However, in his arrogance, Ravana had overlooked asking for protection against humans and animals. So the great god Vishnu, preserver of life on earth, descended from heaven and was born as a mortal prince called Rama. When Rama came of age at sixteen, he set off bravely into the world to vanquish the mighty Ravana and his army of Rakshasa demons. And he wasn't alone. His devoted brother, Lakshmana, and his beautiful wife, Sita, were his constant companions.

Rama went with Lakshmana and Sita to stay in a bamboo hut in the middle of a forest overrun by Rakshasas. Every night the demons stalked the forest, hunting for a feast of human flesh.

Before long, Ravana's monstrous sister noticed the noble, handsome Rama and was at once filled with longing – not to eat him, but to marry him! The hideous creature was filled with jealousy of Sita and one night swooped down to kill her … but they were ready. Rama threw himself in front of his beloved wife, protecting her from the attacking fangs and talons. With one swift movement, Lakshmana drew his sword and sliced off the demoness' nose and ears. Clutching her bloody face, she flew away, screaming in agony.

In the distance, Rama, Lakshmana and Sita heard the horrifying screeching of a demon army preparing to attack. The demoness' brothers had ordered a force of thousands of Rakshasas to avenge their mutilated sister. Rama ordered Lakshmana to take Sita to a safe cave and protect her. Then Rama swiftly donned his helmet and armour, and stood in readiness to take on the swarms of demon warriors by himself.

Never since has such a hero fought such a battle. Many of the gods themselves came down from heaven to watch the prince slay their enemies single-handedly. In a blur of gleaming steel and spraying blood, Rama stood firm, without fear in his heart, and fought long and hard. Soon, the forest floor was covered with dead demon bodies. He defeated every last one.

When the demon king heard about the injuries inflicted on his sister, the death of his brothers, and the total destruction of his army, he was filled with furious outrage and hatred. "Torture and death are too good for that despicable wretch, Rama!" Ravana spat. "I can inflict far more pain on him than that." His eyes sparkled with evil as a plan began to hatch in his mind. "I shall destroy all the things he holds most dear – beginning with his precious wife Sita." Leaping into his magic chariot, Ravana cracked his whip and sped off through the skies towards the forest.

Meanwhile, in the depths of the forest, Rama, Lakshmana and Sita were wandering through the trees when they glimpsed an amazing gold-and-silver deer.

"How wonderful!" Sita exclaimed. "I would love to have that beautiful animal as a pet!"

"Then of course I shall catch it for you," promised Rama.

But Lakshmana was worried. "I have never before seen such a creature. It could be a demon trick," he warned.

"Then you must look after Sita while I am away," Rama instructed.

The prince drew a magic circle of protection all around his wife. "No matter what happens, do not step out of this ring," he told Sita, solemnly. Kissing her tenderly, he crept away through the bushes.

Lakshmana and Sita waited patiently in the dappled sunshine, listening to the leaves rustle and watching the flowers dance. Then suddenly, they heard a loud cry of pain in the distance.

"It's Rama – I'm sure of it!" Sita gasped. "He must be hurt. Lakshmana, go to him at once – please!"

"I'll return as quickly as I can," the prince said, anxiously. And he, too, disappeared into the undergrowth.

Sita stood all alone, wringing her hands with worry. She was so preoccupied that she didn't notice a wrinkly old man approaching until he was almost upon her.

"Alms for a priest?" he begged, holding out a cracked wooden dish. "A gift of food or charity, and I shall pray for your soul," he implored.

Sita was taken completely unawares. She instantly walked over to where the companions' food bag lay on the grass to find something to offer. But the moment Sita moved out of the magic circle, the holy man transformed into the terrible demon king Ravana. Lakshmana had been right – the deer had been a demon in disguise, and the cry of pain had been from a demon mimicking Rama's voice – it was all a trick!

Before Sita could even scream, Ravana grabbed her, flung her into his chariot and raced away like the wind to his distant kingdom.

When the horrified Rama and Lakshmana discovered that Sita was missing, they searched the forest for any trace of her, but there was none. In desperation, Rama asked for help from Sugriva, the cunning king of the monkeys. Sugriva was honoured to be approached by the noble hero. He immediately pledged the best efforts of his people to the prince and despatched his subjects in all four directions to search the world for Sita.

After many days searching, the swift Hanuman, son of the wind, finally tracked Ravana's dark palace down to a mountain at the ends of the earth. Then Hanuman summoned the monkeys into a formidable army under Rama, and roused them to fight.

The battle for Sita raged for many days and nights. Streams of blood flooded the earth. Clouds of dust raised by the warriors blotted out the skies. The thunder of charging chariots could be heard rumbling in countries across the seas. Finally, Rama came face to face with his enemy Ravana. In terror, the sun turned pale, the winds ceased to blow, and the mountains trembled.

Ravana swung at Rama with swords and spears. His army of twenty arms attacked the hero from every angle. But after much bloodshed, the great Rama prevailed, shattering Ravana's black heart with an arrow.

At last, Rama was reunited with his beloved Sita. Lakshmana, Hanuman, and the brave monkey warriors joined them to celebrate the victory of good over evil. And the joyous gods sent down a rain of blossoms from the heavens, covering them with happiness.

Jason and the Argonauts

■ **According to ancient Greek myth**, Jason was a prince of Iolcus who was exiled from his home as a child when his uncle seized the throne.

■ **A wise centaur called Chiron** brought up Jason with other abandoned future heroes, including the mighty warriors Achilles and Aeneas.

■ **The centaur Chiron gave Jason his name**, which means healer.

■ **Jason returned to Iolcus** to claim his throne. His uncle agreed to give up the throne if Jason travelled to the ends of the earth and brought back a magical Golden Fleece.

■ **Jason built a huge ship** for the voyage, called the *Argo*. The goddess Athene gave him a magic bough for the bow of the ship, which was able to speak words of advice.

■ **The greatest heroes in Greek mythology**, including Heracles, volunteered to help Jason in his task. They became the Argonauts.

■ **Jason and the Argonauts** faced peril after peril on their sea voyage. Homer retold many of these adventures in his epic poem, *Odyssey*.

■ **The beautiful witch** Medea fell in love with Jason. She used her magic to help Jason win the Golden Fleece from its owner and escape. It belonged to the king of Colchis – her own father.

▲ *One hazard
encountered by Jason and the
Argonauts on their voyage was the
Symplegades. These were rocks which clashed
together, crushing ships passing between them.*

■ **The name Medea** means cunning. She helped the Argonauts escape by killing her own brother.

■ **Jason later left Medea,** breaking an oath to the gods. This brought trouble upon him. Some said that Medea murdered him in revenge. Others believed that he died an old beggar man.

Sigurd the Volsung

- **Different versions of the legend** of the warrior hero Sigurd the Volsung exist in Norse, British and German mythologies.

- **The earliest existing written version** appears as part of the Norse epic poem *Beowulf*, where a storyteller recites the saga as entertainment for some warrior nobles.

- **The most detailed version** of the myth is known as *The Volsunga Saga*, which was written around AD 1300 by an unknown author.

- **The legend is a superb adventure** story about heroic deeds, magic, love, betrayal, jealousy, danger and death.

- **Volsung is the king of Hunland**, and great-grandson of the Norse father of the gods Odin.

- **Volsung's son, Sigmund**, was also a mighty warrior. In an episode that parallels the legend of the young King Arthur pulling the sword from the stone, Sigmund is the only man who can pull Odin's sword out of an oak tree trunk.

- **Odin favoured Sigmund's son**, the hero Sigurd. Odin helps Sigurd choose a horse that is related to his own magical steed.

- **Odin's sword was smashed** when Sigmund died. Sigurd has the fragments recast into a fearsome weapon called Gram.

- **Sigurd's first quest** is to find a hoard of dwarf gold, guarded by a dragon. One of the treasures is a cursed ring. This inspired J R R Tolkien in *The Lord of the Rings* and also the composer Wagner in his series of operas, *The Ring of the Nibelung*.

- **The saga also contains** an early version of *Beauty and the Beast*.

▼ *The 19th-century German composer Richard Wagner developed several operas, including* The Ring of the Nibelung, *which is based on Sigurd and his adventures.*

The Curse of Andvari's Ring

A Norse myth

It often pleased Odin, the chief of the gods, to disguise himself with a broad-brimmed hat and travelling cloak, and go wandering through Midgard to see all that was happening in the world of men. For one such journey, Odin was accompanied by his brother, Hoenir, and the troublemaker Loki. The three were strolling along, following the course of the river when they saw an otter basking in the sun, eating salmon. The quick and cunning Loki instantly snatched up a stone and threw it at the otter, aiming perfectly and knocking it dead. "Aha!" he cried, triumphantly. "Two prizes with a single shot – and just in time for lunch!"

It wasn't long before Loki was skinning the otter, while Hoenir built a fire and Odin roasted the salmon. Before the gods had tasted even a

morsel of their meal, a very small,
but very furious, man appeared
from over a craggy ledge and
strode towards them. As he
approached, he drew his gleaming sword
and brandished it threateningly. "I am Hreidmar, King of
the Dwarves, and I demand vengeance!" he roared,
purple-faced with rage.

The gods leapt to their feet at once in alarm. "Vengeance?"
Hoenir protested, "but we have done nothing to offend you."

"Nothing!" spat the king. "Nothing! You call slaughtering one
of my sons nothing!" And Hreidmar pointed to the otter skin
dangling from Loki's hand.

The gods looked at each other in horror. They realized at once
what had happened. Dwarves knew very strong magic and some of
them could even change shape and take on animal form. The gods
thought that Loki had killed an otter, but in fact it was a dwarf
prince.

Two burly dwarves came running up behind Hreidmar, one
clutching a stone axe and the other with a dagger.

"My remaining sons, Fafnir and Regin, will have justice!"
Hreidmar thundered, as the men advanced.

"You will forfeit a life for the life you have taken!" one
bellowed.

"Who will pay the price for murdering our brother?" the other raged, edging closer.

"Wait a moment!" cried Odin, thinking fast. "You will gain nothing from killing any of us. However, you will profit well if we pay you compensation instead. It is true that we have grievously wronged you. Now tell us, what is the price of making amends?"

Hreidmar lifted his hand, halting Fafnir and Regin in their tracks. The dwarves turned to each other and consulted for a minute or two. With a greedy smile, Hreidmar nodded. "So be it. You shall bring enough gold to fill the skin of the otter that was once my beloved son, and to cover it entirely. Choose one of you to go and fetch the gold. The other two must remain here as our hostages." Hreidmar grinned as the otter skin grew larger and larger before their very eyes.

"I will go," Loki volunteered, relishing the chance to outdo the tricksters. "I know where there is a trove of treasure so large, it should easily satisfy your needs – although it will take all the cunning I possess if I am to lay my hands on it." Without a moment's delay, he sped off, leaving Odin and Hoenir at the mercy of the dwarves.

Loki knew that for his plan to work, he would have to beg for the help of the giants – sworn enemies of the gods. He needed a favour from Ran, the cold-hearted wife of the giant who ruled the sea. Loki wanted to borrow Ran's enchanted fishing net, which she

used to catch shipwrecked sailors and drown them in the deeps.
Fortunately, only because Loki was half-giant, Ran grudgingly
agreed.

Next, Loki journeyed to a place where a mighty waterfall
thundered over a towering cliff into a plunging pool – the home of
another dwarf, Andvari. Although Loki had had enough dealings
with dwarves to last him a lifetime, he knew of no one else to turn
to. Andvari was believed to have a secret treasure trove, as large as

the highest mountain. Keeping his fingers crossed, Loki just hoped that the rumours were true …

Loki settled himself by the side of the pool and used his power to blend his body into the landscape. An unseeing mouse ran over his foot. An unnoticing butterfly came and settled on his nose. But not once did Loki stir. He just sat … and watched … and waited. At last he saw a trout that was bigger and shinier than all the other fish. Swifter than a darting kingfisher, he cast Ran's net, ensnared the trout, and drew it spluttering and flapping onto the bank. Grabbing it, Loki squeezed as hard as he could, until suddenly the trout changed shape – into the dwarf, Andvari!

"Stop! Stop!" Andvari gasped. "Tell me what you want and stop squashing the life out of me!"

Easing his grip a little, Loki made his demands. The dwarf was outraged, but imprisoned in Loki's clutches, he had no choice. Fuming, he directed Loki up a secret pathway behind the waterfall, to a

cave that was filled from floor to ceiling with an incredible sight –
gold. Gold cups, gold crowns, gold coins, gold necklaces, gold
rings, gold bracelets, gold earrings, gold weapons, gold belts, gold
brooches – a million and one golden objects glistened and
gleamed in the darkness. With his eyes wide, Loki said "I need it
all – and I mean all."

Sulking, Andvari helped Loki to pack up all his treasure, until
there was no sign that the gold had ever been
there. "That's it," Andvari sighed,
mournfully. "I've given you everything."

"Not quite everything," corrected
Loki, reaching out for a ring on Andvari's
little finger.

"Please, I beseech you!" Andvari begged.
"I've given you all the gold I have. Allow me to
keep this one small ring. It contains the charm I need
to make more gold – but I swear to you that the magic will not
work for anyone other than me."

"I told you," Loki insisted firmly, pulling the ring off the
dwarf's hand and slipping it into his pocket. "I need it all."

"Then have it!" cried the devastated dwarf. "And may a curse of
sorrow be on it for ever more! May wretchedness, misery and
death come to whoever wears it!" Andvari would have continued,
but Loki and the treasure were already gone.

When Odin and Hoenir saw Loki returning with the enormous hoard of gold, they were mightily relieved. Eagerly, King Hreidmar and his sons watched as the three gods stuffed the otter skin until it was almost bursting, and carefully covered it, bit by bit. At last, all the gold was used up and the gods were done – or so they thought.

"Not so fast!" cried Hreidmar. "There is one hair on the otter's nose still showing. Either give up more gold or give up your lives!"

Luckily, Loki remembered Andvari's ring. "Take this with my pleasure," he smirked, throwing the band of bad luck onto the pile. And the gods gladly left the dwarves admiring their newfound wealth.

This is only the start of the curse of the ring. In the end, Fafnir and Regin murdered their father to keep the treasure for themselves. They argued and Fafnir banished Regin – who found the means to have his brother murdered, before he was himself slain. And so the ring passed on from hand to hand, bringing sorrow, wretchedness, misery and death to whoever wore it – just as Andvari had desired.

Gilgamesh

■ **This epic poem** is from Sumeria – one of the earliest civilizations to have city states, laws and irrigation.

■ **Gilgamesh was a real king** of the Sumerian city Uruk, around 2700–2500 BC.

■ **In the poem**, King Gilgamesh is a man of mighty strength who is loved dearly by the gods.

■ **When the nobles of Uruk** complain to the gods that King Gilgamesh is a tyrant, the mother goddess makes a hero called Enkidu to challenge him. Gilgamesh meets his match in Enkidu, but the two soon become friends.

■ **When Enkidu dies**, Gilgamesh begins to fear his own death. He embarks on a quest to find out how to become immortal.

▶ *Gilgamesh was a powerful and oppressive king in ancient Sumeria. He battles fearsome creatures, such as the giant Humbaba, in order to create a lasting legend of himself.*

▶ *The Sumerians developed the first alphabet about 5000 years ago. Each of the 600 markings represent a word or part of a word. Gilgamesh was first recorded on clay tablets.*

■ **Gilgamesh does not win eternal life**, but is rewarded with a plant to keep him young and strong for the rest of his days. When a watersnake steals it from him, he sinks into despair.

■ **Gilgamesh finally realizes** that the only type of immortality humans can achieve is fame through performing great deeds.

■ **The poem was discovered** in 1845, when archaeologists were excavating at the ancient city of Nineveh.

■ **Experts think that** *Gilgamesh* was first written down on clay tablets in an ancient language called cuneiform. It is the earliest recorded major work of literature.

■ **Fragments of** *Gilgamesh* have been found by archaeologists in ancient sites throughout many countries in the Middle East.

Gilgamesh and Humbaba

From the epic poem *Gilgamesh*

Gilgamesh was a mighty king, ruler of the great city of Uruk. His father, Lugalbanda, had been a noble king before him and his mother was the wise goddess Ninsun. Gilgamesh was especially favoured by the gods. The great mother goddess Nintu had helped to create him. The sun god Shamash had bestowed beauty upon him. The storm god Adad had filled him with courage. The god of learning and intelligence Ea had given him wisdom. Indeed, Gilgamesh had been granted many divine gifts, but he had not been given the gift he prized most of all – immortality. Gilgamesh was human, and like all humans, he would eventually die.

One day, Gilgamesh was sitting with his dearest friend, the warrior Enkidu, when he declared, "Before I die, I want to win a place among the greatest heroes who have ever lived. Then, people will tell tales of my glorious deeds for thousands of years to come, and my name shall live on through the ages."

"O great Gilgamesh," Enkidu replied, "you are already a renowned ruler of a powerful people and a magnificent city, admired throughout the land. How do you intend to achieve even greater fame? Surely you are as famous as you can be!"

Gilgamesh paused. There was an excited gleam in his eyes. He announced, "I am going to slay the giant, Humbaba!"

Enkidu gasped. "Tell me you are not serious!

Everyone who has heard of Humbaba quakes in fear at his name! Humbaba has a ferocious face like a great dragon, a terrifying roar like a rampaging river, gnashing teeth like a bloodthirsty lion, and fiery breath that scorches everything in his path. The divine ruler Enlil appointed Humbaba to scare travellers away from the mountain home of the gods, which lies in the deep, dark Cedar Forest of Lebanon – so wild and treacherous that you can enter it and never find your way out again."

"All that is true," smiled Gilgamesh. "Nevertheless, I am determined to track this monster down and slay him! The whole world will talk of my adventure. Say you will come with me, Enkidu."

Enkidu shook his head. "My lord, I am not yet ready to die," he exclaimed.

"Come, Enkidu," coaxed Gilgamesh, "would you rather wait for death to find you, or go and greet it face to face. I am going to slay Humbaba. Poets will sing forever of Gilgamesh, King of Uruk!"

Enkidu sighed. "My king, if your mind is made up, then I shall remain at your side until the very end."

Gilgamesh hurried off to prepare. First, he made a sacrifice at the temple of Shamash. "O radiant one," he begged, "take pity on my mortality. Help me to conquer Humbaba and win everlasting fame."

Then Gilgamesh called the elders of Uruk to a meeting and told them of his plan. They were horrified and protested angrily, but Gilgamesh was defiant and could not be persuaded otherwise.

Finally, he told his mother of his plans. She wept and wailed, and prayed to the gods to change his mind. But finally, she kissed Gilgamesh and Enkidu goodbye. "Go forth with my blessing, but return safely home to me."

Gilgamesh took the bravest warriors of Uruk, along with supplies and weapons, including an axe especially forged by his smiths for felling Humbaba. Then Enkidu led the way out of the gates of Uruk and down the road that led towards Humbaba's lair.

To reach the gateway to the Cedar Forest of Lebanon, it should have taken six weeks. However, with motivated hearts, Gilgamesh, Enkidu and the warriors covered the distance in three days. Before they entered the gloom of the woods, Gilgamesh gave a speech.

"No one who follows me should be afraid. If we die, we die making lasting names for ourselves. We will not disappear into the well of time and be forgotten, like cowards. So be of good courage and let us go forward together!"

"Gilgamesh's dreams prophesy victory!" announced Enkidu. "Our mighty god Shamash will help us, and we will triumph over the greatest of giants, Humbaba!"

Then Gilgamesh, Enkidu and their brave army plunged determinedly into the forest, their hearts pounding. They marched all day into its depths, before Gilgamesh gave the order to stop. He took out his axe and began cutting down one of the massive cedars – a bold ploy to attract Humbaba's attention.

In the silence of the forest, the thudding chops resounded like the beat of a battle drum. As the tree finally toppled and fell, the warriors saw bursts of flame in the distance and heard huge footsteps striding towards them. Humbaba's thunderous voice struck terror into their hearts. "Who dares enter my forest and cut down the trees of the heavenly mountain of the gods? Answer me and prepare to die!"

"I, Gilgamesh, King of Uruk, have felled your tree," Gilgamesh bellowed back, "and now I will fell you with my mighty axe!"

Gilgamesh brandished his axe overhead and charged forwards to meet the oncoming monster. Enkidu roared a mighty battle cry, and he and the warriors followed suit. As they did so, Shamash rewarded their courage by sending mighty winds from heaven against Humbaba. The blasts beat upon him from all directions and hurled him backwards through the forest, until he was held trapped against the wall of his own house.

The huge giant thrashed and struggled, but remained pinned to the wall by the force of the wind. Quivering and quaking with fear, he cried, "Have mercy, great Gilgamesh. I swear that if you let me live, I shall become your faithful servant."

But Enkidu shook his head sternly. "Do not listen to the cunning creature," he advised. "If you set him free, you will surely never see Uruk again."

Gilgamesh listened to his friend's wise words. Raising his axe high above his head, he struck Humbaba with all his might. The giant's body hit the ground with an almighty thud, which echoed throughout the great forest for many miles.

Gilgamesh, Enkidu and the warriors returned triumphant to Uruk – not only with the head of Humbaba, but with many felled cedars to make the mighty city of Uruk even stronger.

Gilgamesh's faith in himself paid off. He got his wish and tales are still told of his courageous deed to this very day.

The adventures of Theseus

■ **There are many myths** about a hero called Theseus who became king of Attica in Greece. Historians have proved that a real King Theseus did once exist.

■ **According to legends**, Theseus was the secret son of King Aegeus. Theseus was brought up away from Attica, to keep him safe from enemies who wanted the throne for themselves.

■ **As a young man**, Theseus travelled to Attica to claim his birthright. He chose a long route through many dangers because he wanted to prove himself on the way.

■ **Theseus once took a mighty bronze-plated club** from a thug who tried to kill him. He used the weapon for the rest of his life.

■ **Criminals were often punished by Theseus** using their own evil methods. One villain that he encountered tied people between two bent young trees, which then sprang back and ripped them apart. Theseus did the same to the villain.

■ **When Theseus reached Attica**, his stepmother tried to poison him. Luckily King Aegeus recognized his son just in time.

◄ *Many myths have developed about the Minotaur, which was half-man, half-bull. It was imprisoned in a maze by King Minos of Crete. When locked in the maze to meet certain death, Theseus defeated the terrifying monster.*

▲ *It is thought that Theseus built the city of Athens. The ruins of the Parthenon, a temple to the goddess, Athene, still stands today.*

■ **Each year, Aegeus had to send** young people as human sacrifices to King Minos of Crete. Brave Theseus volunteered to go. He was thrown into a maze called the Labyrinth to be eaten by a ferocious bull-headed man, the Minotaur. Instead, Theseus slew the monster.

■ **King Minos' daughter** Ariadne fell in love with Theseus and helped him to escape from the Labyrinth.

■ **Archaeologists have found** that the ancient royal palace of Crete was laid out like a maze, and that a dangerous sport similar to bull-fighting was very popular. The myth of the Minotaur might have arisen from stories about them.

■ **Historians credit Theseus** with building Athens as an important Greek centre of power. Today it is the capital of the country.

Cuchulain

■ **Cuchulain (pronounced Cu-hoo-lin) was a warrior hero** supposed to have lived in Ireland in the first century AD.

■ **Stories say that Cuchulain** was born when the king of Ulster's sister was magically swept away by the god Lugh. However, the baby's name was originally Setanta.

■ **Setanta was schooled** by the greatest heroes and poets at the king of Ulster's court.

■ **As a teenager**, Setanta single-handedly killed a ferocious dog belonging to the blacksmith, Culan. This is how he got his nickname because Cuchulain means 'Hound of Culan'.

■ **Once, Cuchulain overheard Cathbad the Druid** phophesy that anyone who became a warrior that day would become the most famous hero in all Ireland – but would die young. Cuchulain was 15, but decided to arm himself to fulfil the prophecy.

◀ *The Celts believed that the goddess of death, Badb, often appeared at battlefields in the form of a raven. According to one legend, a raven drank the blood of the wounded Cuchulain as he fought heroically to his death.*

▶ *Berserkirs were warriors who worked themselves into a frenzied trance before battle. Wearing animal skins, they charged at the enemy howling like wolves. They were feared as wild and dangerous animals on the battlefield.*

■ **Cuchulain wanted a short, glorious life** rather than a longer, more unremarkable one.

■ **As a berserk warrior**, Cuchulain was frenzied in battle and terrifying to behold. Power sparked from his hair, his body hissed with heat, his eyes bulged, his muscles stretched his skin, and blood frothed on his lips.

■ **By defeating the tricks of a cunning chieftain** called Forgal the Wily, Cuchulain won his wife, Emer.

■ **In the end, Cuchulain died in battle.** He was fatally wounded, but lashed himself to a standing stone, so he would die on his feet, fighting to the end.

■ **Cathbad the Druid's prediction** came true because in Irish mythology, Cuchulain is considered to be the greatest of all Irish warrior heroes.

The Hound of Culan

An Irish legend

Midway through chieftain Sualtim's wedding day, his beautiful young bride, Dechtire, mysteriously disappeared. Sualtim's advisors sought her high and low, but to no avail. It was as if she had vanished into thin air. At first, Sualtim was furious. It had not been an easy job persuading King Conor of Ulster to let him marry his sister. But finally he had won the hand of the fairest woman in the land and secured an alliance with the most powerful ruler in all of Erin. Now, it seemed that Dechtire had run away, ruining not just his romance but also his political plans. However, Amergin the wise Druid advised Sualtim not to be too hasty. Amergin could sense ancient magic in the air … and what could humans do against the will of the almighty gods?

So Sualtim waited patiently and a whole year passed by, until one day Dechtire came walking out of the forest, carrying a baby in her arms. She told Sualtim an amazing story … the heroic god Lugh swooped down on the day of her marriage to Sualtim and whisked her off to the Land of Fairy. Lugh was also the father of the child that she held so tenderly in her arms.

Sualtim was in a quandary. If Dechtire had borne a child by another mortal, he would have hunted the man down, slashed off his head and paraded it for all to see. However, as Amergin pointed out, Sualtim had been paid a great honour by the gods. So, from the moment Sualtim laid eyes on the child, he thought of him as his own and brought him up as his rightful heir.

Many thought that Sualtim was foolish for believing Dechtire's wild tale. But as time went on, even the most hardened sceptics began to think that perhaps her story was true.

The child, who Dechtire named Setanta, was markedly different from other children. He began to walk before most children his age could even crawl. He learned to read before other children could speak. When he started lessons, he showed an attentiveness and intelligence that surprised all his teachers. By the age of only eight, Setanta spoke with the thoughtfulness of Amergin himself, and could hold his own in combat with the fastest, strongest, most experienced of Sualtim's warriors.

Sualtim often thought that his chest would burst with love and pride when he watched his adopted son. But he also realized that he had already taught Setanta all he had to offer. "You will always be my son," he told the boy tenderly, "but you were borne of the god Lugh and you are clearly destined for greatness. If you wish to learn more, you must go to the very best in the land – to the court of your uncle, King Conor. Be wary of him as he is cunning and slippery, and will wish to avoid his duty to you. But, my golden son, I have no doubt that you will find a way to win him over."

On the day Setanta arrived at the king's fortress in Emain Macha, the men and women of the court were out watching their sons compete in an annual hurley match. As Setanta joined the cheering crowd of spectators, he immediately saw a way to get the attention of the king.

Grabbing a spare hurley stick, he ran out to join the game, tackling the player with the ball and siezing it from him with great skill. Then he set off down the pitch, swiftly sprinting past the players, dodging between them or shouldering them out of the way as they came out to tackle him – all the while with the ball dancing at the end of his stick. By the time Setanta reached the goal, the players were left motionless, totally dumbfounded, while the crowd were roaring and leaping about with delight. Setanta smashed the ball through the goalkeeper's legs and the crowd went wild!

"Tell that boy to come here at once, whoever he is!" roared the stunned King Conor. "I will not have people just waltzing in here, without my permission." However, when he found out that the extraordinarily talented hurley player was in fact his nephew, he was pleased to claim him as his own kin.

From then on, Setanta was instructed in the arts and skills of a noble warrior by the finest teachers of the court. And it became one of King Conor's greatest pleasures to show Setanta to all the chieftains who owed him allegiance.

Once, when Setanta was a teenager, the king asked the lad to accompany him to the home of Culan, the master blacksmith. However, as Setanta was playing hurling, he told his uncle not to wait for him, and he would follow on later.

By the time Setanta had finished his game and arrived at the home of Culan, the warriors were inside feasting, and the gates were closed.

Pacing the grounds was Culan's enormous, drooling guard dog, renowned for being a bloodthirsty, vicious maneater. Spotting Setanta, the brute bounded towards him, growling and barking ferociously. Without a moment's hesitation, Setanta drew out his hurley stick and ball. Taking perfect aim, he struck the hound directly between the eyes. The creature keeled over dead before it had even sniffed a hair on Setanta's head.

Culan heard the commotion and came rushing out, his sword at the ready. He was truly astonished at the sight of Setanta standing unharmed over the body of the beast – and somewhat annoyed that he was now without a guard dog!

"Until you find and raise another hound, I will be your guard dog and keep watch at your fortress," promised Setanta.

And that is how Setanta became known as Cuchulain, meaning 'the hound of Culan'. The blacksmith's guard dog was only the first of many monsters Cuchulain vanquished. Witches, magicians and creatures of evil that faced him met certain death.

Whenever Cuchulain went into battle, a strange frenzy came over him, which was terrifying to behold. And in all the time from those ancient days to the present, there has never been a greater hero in the land of Erin.

Lugh, the Master of Masters

An Irish legend

Thousands of years ago, there lived in Ireland a people descended from the goddess Dana. Beautiful and honourable, they were highly skilled in all arts – including the art of war. However, no one – not even King Nuada himself – was strong enough to withstand the evil Fomorian raiders from the lands across the sea. The King of the Fomorians was Balor of the Evil Eye – for one eye was all he had, but whoever it turned upon was instantly struck down dead. Feared throughout the land, the Fomorians were evil giants who wreaked havoc upon the people of Ireland. The formidable Balor concealed the power of his evil eye with a gigantic brass eyepatch.

However, when he wished doom upon his enemies, four men heaved ropes and pulleys to hoist the mighty eye-shield open, and woe betide anyone who happened to be within his line of sight.

King Nuada and his people had no choice but to give in to the demands of Balor and the Fomorians – a tax on every stone for grinding wheat, a tax on every kneading trough for mixing dough, a tax on every oven used to bake bread, and a tax of one ounce of gold for every man in Ireland. Yet still the Fomorians often descended upon the countryside, plundering and pillaging.

The People of Dana were in despair with absolutely no hope left … until one day when a stranger came knocking at the high gates of King Nuada's fortress. With a divine quality about him, the stranger's face shone like the sun.

"Who are you?" demanded the gatekeeper, warily. "What do you want here?"

"I am Lugh, a mighty warrior," the stranger said.

"The mightiest warriors of Ireland are here," the gatekeeper replied.

"I am a fine blacksmith and carpenter," Lugh declared.

"The finest blacksmiths and carpenters of Ireland are here," the gatekeeper sneered.

"I am a skilled poet and musician," Lugh said, undetered.

"The most skilled poets and musicians of Ireland are here," the gatekeeper boasted.

"I am a powerful healer and magician," Lugh continued.

"The most powerful healers and magicians of Ireland are here," the gatekeeper insisted.

"If your people are masters of all these arts," Lugh countered, "they will not fear to pit themselves against me."

At this bold challenge, the gatekeeper hurried to King Nuada.

The king was intrigued. "We will put this stranger to the test. Let him in," he decided.

Lugh was finally allowed inside, but not beyond the outer courtyard. Firstly, he had to play a game of fidchell, which is rather like chess. Lugh beat every opponent in fewer moves than anyone had ever seen before. Then, he had to compete against a strongman called Ogma, in lifting and throwing an enormous flagstone. Ogma tossed the flagstone right across the courtyard. However, Lugh hurled the flagstone right out of the courtyard, over the towering fortress wall. Finally, the best storytellers told tales of the adventures of heroes – each one held their audience rapt, eager for more. When Lugh's turn came, he played sweet harp music and sang beautiful melodies with such stirring words that energy and hope pulsed through the people, in a way that they had never experienced before. The amazed crowd agreed that Lugh truly was the master of masters!

At last, Lugh was led to meet King Nuada himself.

"Honour us by telling us who you are," the king asked.

"My name is Lugh," the hero declared. "I am of the People of Dana, but I was brought up by the fairies and instructed in the ways of magic. My boat is called *Wave-Sweeper*. It knows my mind and goes wherever I wish it, swifter than the wind. My sword is named *The Answerer*. It cuts its way through iron of any thickness. I offer myself at your service."

At that moment, a commotion at the entrance to the throne room disturbed them. Lugh span round to see a rough band of giant Fomorian thugs striding in.

"You owe us taxes," their leader snarled, spitting on the king. "Fetch them now or we will slay your people one by one."

Lugh was outraged. "How dare you talk to the great King Nuada like this – and in his own throne room!" he roared.

The Fomorians didn't utter a sound. All except one of them had their throats slit by Lugh – he had drawn *The Answerer* and slashed them too quickly for anyone to see. The heads of the giants crashed to the floor, followed shortly after by their collapsed bodies. The remaining Fomorian stood aghast, trembling in shock.

"Be gone, back to that abomination Balor." Lugh bellowed. "Tell him that the next head to fall will be his own."

With that, the thug sped from the throne room, dodging kicks and blows that rained down on him from the cheering People of Dana.

The triumphant King Nuada wasted no time in making Lugh head of the war council. Lugh prepared the warriors for battle, while he himself rode into the west to ask the fairies for help. Meanwhile, as Lugh and the king expected, the furious Balor summoned his own wicked forces and headed for Ireland.

The day soon came when a great war shook the earth of Ireland – the Fomorian giants set all their strength against the valorous People of Dana. Rivers of blood flowed through the land and bodies piled high on the battlefield. But the Irish chiefs held their own, protected by the powerful magic of the fairies.

When Balor gave the command for his evil eye to be opened, Lugh was ready. He loaded a slingshot with a stone and fired it straight into the giant's eye. Hitting its target with such force, the stone blasted Balor's eye right through the back of his enormous head. It span through the air, killing every giant it passed over.

By the time dusk fell, victory belonged to King Nuada. Ireland was saved and the people sing of the hero Lugh to this very day.

Mythological monsters

- **Myths from the Aborigines** of Australia tell of a swamp monster called the Bunyip that hunts children at night.

- **In Greek mythology**, the Sphinx had a woman's face, a lion's body, and a bird's wings. It killed travellers who could not work out its riddles.

- **Many Scandinavian myths** feature hairy, cruel creatures called trolls that live inside the earth and are expert metalworkers.

- **Greek stories say that a manticore** had a lion's body, but a human face – with three rows of teeth. It shot poisoned spines from its tail.

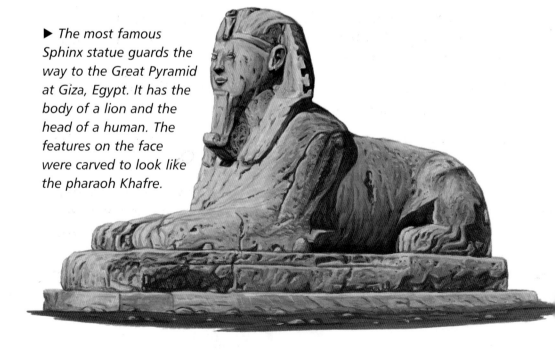

▶ *The most famous Sphinx statue guards the way to the Great Pyramid at Giza, Egypt. It has the body of a lion and the head of a human. The features on the face were carved to look like the pharaoh Khafre.*

▶ *After the Norse hero Beowulf kills the monster Grendel, Grendel's mother emerges from her lake and attacks the great hall, Heorot. Beowulf hunts her down and beheads her with a mighty sword.*

■ **The Hound of the Baskervilles** by Victorian writer Sir Arthur Conan Doyle has become a modern myth about a gigantic hound from hell.

■ **According to German legend**, monsters shaped like beautiful women called Lorelei sat on jagged rocks in the river Rhine. If fishermen listened to their enchanting songs, they died in the fast-flowing waters on the rocks.

■ **In Greek myth**, the chimaera was a fire-breathing monster with a lion's head, a goat's body and a serpent's tail.

■ **A gryphon was a cross** between a lion and an eagle, which first appeared in myths of the Middle East.

■ **A basilisk, or cockatrice**, appears in the Bible, as well as Greek legend. It was a snake with a cockerel's wings and a dragon's tail. J K Rowling featured the monster in *Harry Potter and the Chamber of Secrets*.

■ **Medusa the Gorgon was a female monster** in Greek myth with writhing snakes for hair. Anyone who looked at her face turned to stone.

Mysterious places

■ **Aborigines believe that the land** is filled with spirits. Uluru, or Ayers Rock, in central Australia is one of the most holy places.

■ **Stonehenge is a circle of standing stones** in Wiltshire, England, dating from around 2800 BC. The stones were arranged so that the sun shone into the entranceway on the morning of the summer solstice.

■ **Since the 1980s**, crop circles have been appearing in wheat fields throughout Britain. Some say that they are the work of alien visitors.

■ **Over 200 ships and planes** have vanished in an area off Florida called the Bermuda Triangle. Some believe that strange energies exist here.

■ **Many myths have developed** around a reported UFO crash near Roswell, USA, in 1947. Film footage of aliens has even emerged – although this has never been proved to be genuine or fake.

▼ *Ancient gigantic figures on Easter Island were carved from volcanic rock and erected facing the sea.*

▲ *Uluru, or Ayers Rock, in central Australia is a huge rock of sandstone that is 335 m in height. Aborigines hold religious ceremonies there to make contact with ancestor spirits from the Dreamtime.*

■ **At Carnac in France**, thousands of huge stones are arranged in parallel rows. No one knows which ancient people put them there or why.

■ **In 1927, a pilot discovered enormous line drawings** etched into the Nazca plains, Peru. Although no one knows why, archaeologists think they were created 1000–2500 years ago.

■ **Dozens of giant stone statues** stand on Easter Island in the Pacific Ocean, probably made from AD 1000–1500. They may represent the guardian spirits of the islanders' ancestors.

■ **Some people believe** that the 1969 *Apollo II* mission when Neil Armstrong was the first human to walk on the moon, was a myth made up by USA officials. The event could have been filmed in the Nevada desert at a location called Area 51, which remains a top secret government zone to this day.

■ **Varanasi is a city in India** on the banks of the river Ganges. Hindus believe that anyone who washes in the waters will go straight to heaven when they die.

Magical possessions

■ **The Chinese spirit, Monkey**, had a deadly iron fighting stick that could change magically into a tiny needle, for keeping behind his ear.

■ **King Arthur wielded the mighty sword**, Excalibur, given to him by a strange spirit called the Lady of the Lake.

■ **The mighty Norse thunder god**, Thor, had a throwing hammer, Mjollnir, which never missed its target, and a belt, Meginjardir, which doubled his superhuman strength.

■ **The Celtic hero Lugh** had a boat called *Wave-Sweeper* that could travel over land and sea, and a sword called the Answerer that could cut through anything.

■ **According to Bible stories**, the prophet Moses had a staff that god enabled to work magic, rather like a wand.

■ **In the Indian epic *Ramayana***, Prince Rama possessed the god Vishnu's bow, Brahma's shining arrows, and Indra's quiver to keep them in.

▶ *When King Arthur was dying, he ordered Sir Bedivere to throw Excalibur back into the lake it came from. A hand rose from the waters to claim it.*

▲ *The prophet Moses used his magic staff to help the Israelites escape from slavery in Egypt. He wielded power over the Red Sea, and the pursuing Egyptian army was drowned.*

■ **The Norse goddess Freya** owned a spectacular dwarf-crafted necklace called the Brisingamen, and a feather coat that gave the wearer the power of flight.

■ **A Chinese legend tells** how some kind villagers helped the hero Bao Chu by using their own clothes to make him a magic coat. It kept him warm even when he fell into a river of ice.

■ **The Dagda, the chief of a race of Celtic gods** called Tuatha De Danaan, had a magic cauldron that never ran out of food.

■ **Greek myth says that the god** of the underworld, Hades, owned a helmet of invisibility.

Freya and the Brising Necklace

A Norse myth

The beautiful goddess Freya wandered through the halls of her palace, counting her blessings. She had a wonderful husband, the god Odur, and two lovely daughters, as fair as flowers. They had an elegant home and splendid garden in the heavenly realm of Asgard, surrounded by their friends. Still, Freya's heart was restless, yearning for excitement.

Preparing her carriage pulled by cats, she decided to go on a journey. First, she travelled through Midgard to see the world of humans. Then she journeyed through the land of the light elves, Alfheim, home of her dear brother, Frey. Finally, she found herself at the borders of Svartalfheim, the rocky realm of the black dwarves.

A wicked dwarf called Dvalin and his three equally wicked brothers learned that the beautiful goddess was coming and set a trap for her.

Deep inside a dark cave, they
built a workshop and busied
themselves with an anvil,
hammer and a fiery furnace.
As Freya wandered along, the
noise of the dwarves
sparked her curiosity and
she drew closer.

Lit only by a raging furnace,
Freya found four dwarves hard at work.
They pretended not to notice her
arrival. Looking around, she suddenly
caught sight of their anvil and gasped in astonishment. There,
glittering and gleaming in the golden flames, was the most
beautiful necklace she had ever seen. Unbeknown to the
unfortunate Freya, the necklace was enchanted. From the moment
the goddess laid her eyes on it, the charms began to take effect and
she felt an uncontrollable need to possess it.

"You have surely crafted the most exquisite necklace in the
universe," Freya breathed, her heart pounding. "How much silver
do you ask for it?"

"The Brising Necklace is indeed the most desirable adornment
in all creation," Dvalin replied, "but we could not sell it for all the
silver in the world."

Freya's pulse raced. She could not take her eyes off it. "Then how much gold do you ask for it?" she said.

"The Brising Necklace is not for sale for any treasure of gold," Dvalin countered.

Freya began to feel desperate. She could not walk away without it. "There must be some treasure you will take for the necklace," she implored. "Please tell me, what is your price? I am willing to pay whatever you want!"

The dwarf brothers exchanged evil glances. "The only treasure we will exchange for the necklace is you," Dvalin stated firmly. "You must be married to each of us for one day and one night, and in return, the necklace will be yours."

Freya was so enchanted that she did not hesitate. "So be it," she agreed, and the deal was done.

As soon as Freya held the Brising Necklace as her prize, she came to her senses and felt ashamed and guilty. How she regretted betraying her beloved Odur. The only solution was to keep the necklace hidden away, so no one would ever see it and find out what she had done.

Hurrying home to Asgard, she stowed the necklace safely in her chamber, setting strong magic onto the door and window locks so that only she was allowed to enter. Freya breathed a heavy sigh of relief. She never dreamed that anyone would find out about the four dwarf weddings, held deep underground in Svartalfheim. Her secret was safe forever …

However, the mischievous god Loki made it
his unofficial business to find out about everything
that went on in the universe. He soon discovered all
about Freya's misdemeanour and, being the troublemaker
he was, he delighted in telling all to Odur.

Odur was furious, not at Freya, but at Loki. "How dare you
enter my home and accuse my wife of such unfaithfulness,
without a shred of evidence!" Odur roared. "I utterly refuse to
believe it. Unless you can bring me this Brising Necklace as proof,
I shall tear you limb from limb if you cross my path again. Now
get out of my sight!"

Fuming, Loki slunk away. He was determined to make Odur
eat his words by somehow stealing the necklace and showing it to
him. Loki knew that Freya had sealed the chamber with magic, so
trying to break in was out of the question. Instead, he turned
himself into a fly and zipped around the door and windows,
searching for a tiny hole to squeeze through. At last he found one
right at the top of a window seal – it was no bigger than the eye of
a needle, but it was enough.

Holding his breath, Loki wriggled through, and found himself
inside Freya's chamber. There she was, curled up asleep on her
bed, wearing the cursed Brising Necklace. Even Loki had to admit
that it truly was a priceless work. Silently, he turned himself back

into human form, and gently slid the necklace from around her throat. Quietly unlocking the door, he stole away into the night.

When Freya awoke the next morning, finding the necklace gone and her door unlocked, she knew at once that her guilty secret had been discovered. Beside herself with anguish, she hurried to find her husband to confess everything. However, Odur was nowhere to be seen. Freya searched high and low in a panic, but her cherished husband was gone.

Distraught, Freya dashed to the mighty Odin and threw herself at his feet. Weeping bitterly, she told all. "I shall never rest until I find my husband and beg his forgiveness," she sobbed.

Odin looked grave. The all-seeing father of the gods knew all about Freya's sin, and how her estranged husband had stridden away, heartbroken. He also knew where Odur was ... but he decided the goddess had to learn a bitter lesson. "Wander the universe until you find Odur and win his pardon," Odin announced. "But you must wear the necklace forever more, as a permanent reminder of your mistake."

Odin sent the messenger, Heimdall, to retrieve the necklace from Loki, and soon it was clasped around Freya's neck once more.

With a heavy heart, Freya wandered away from Asgard, searching for her husband. Wise Odin watched her go with fondness, knowing that all would soon be well again between them.

Norse world order

■ **Two main written sources** tell us what the Norse people believed about the universe. The Prose Edda is a collection of myths recorded by an Icelander called Snorri Sturluson (1179–1241). The Poetic Edda is a collection of 34 ancient poems recorded in the 17th century.

■ **Many Viking carvings** show pictures of what the Norse people believed the universe to be like.

▼ *According to Norse myth, Ragnarok was the day of doom – a battle between good and evil signalling the end of the world. The giant sea-serpent Jormungand swam ashore to join the battle against the warrior gods.*

▶ *Lucky charms were thought to protect Vikings against evil. An amulet shaped like Thor's hammer was worn by warriors as it was thought to give them extra strength in battle.*

■ **The Norse people thought** there were nine worlds arranged on three levels.

■ **The uppermost worlds were** Alfheim, home of the light elves; Vanaheim, home of the fertility gods; and Asgard, home of the warrior gods.

■ **The middle worlds were** Midgard, home of humans; Nidavellir, home of the dwarves; Jotunheim, home of the giants; and Svartalfheim, home of the black dwarves.

■ **Norse myth said that a giant serpent** called Jormungand lived in the sea surrounding the middle worlds, circling them.

■ **The underworlds were** Muspellheim, a land of fire; and the freezing land of Niflheim, which included Hel, home of the dead.

■ **The Norse warrior gods** remained young and strong by eating the Golden Apples of Youth belonging to the goddess, Iduna. Without these, they would face old age and death.

■ **Characters from the Norse worlds** such as giants, dwarves and elves also found their way into many European fairy tales, such as *The Elves and the Shoemaker*.

■ **Inspiration for the names** in J R R Tolkien's *The Lord of the Rings* trilogy came from characters in the nine Norse worlds.

Stories of the sun

■ **The Inuits were thought to live** in total darkness, until Raven flew to a far-off country and stole them a piece of daylight.

■ **A Chinese myth tells** that there were once ten suns that took it in turns to cross the sky. One day, they all decided to appear together. The earth began to scorch, so the gods commanded an archer called Yi to shoot them all dead, except one.

■ **The Incas sacrificed** honoured young girls to the sun god Inti at the June solstice, the shortest day of the year.

■ **The ancient Egyptians believed** that every day the sun god Ra sailed across the sky in a Boat of Millions of Years. At night, he made a perilous journey through the underworld.

■ **An important centre** for the worship of Ra was Heliopolis, which means 'sun city'.

■ **Many Native American plains tribes** held a yearly sun dance that lasted around four days, usually beginning on the summer solstice. The dances usually included dancing, singing and drumming.

◀ *The Mayan people of Central America made a stone calendar on the ground, in the shape of the sun. The face of the sun god was carved in the middle and signs for the days carved around the outside. Time was tracked by the sun's movement.*

▲ *Many Native American tribes, such as the Blackfoot Native Americans, held an annual sun dance. The dancers aimed to draw the sun's power into themselves.*

■ **Navajo Native Americans believed** that the god, Tsohanoai, carried the sun on his back during the day. At night, he hung it on the wall of his house.

■ **An Indian myth tells** how the sun god Surya was so bright that his wife ran away to live in a shady forest.

■ **Myth says that one grandson** of the sun goddess Amaterasu married the goddess of Mount Fuji, and one of their great-grandchildren became Japan's first emperor.

■ **The Greek sun god Apollo** was also the god of music, prophecy, archery and healing, and the protector of shepherds.

Stories of the stars

▲ *Halley's Comet can be seen once every 75–76 years. It is featured on the 11th-century Bayeux tapestry, which shows the Battle of Hastings in 1066.*

- **Western names for star constellations** come from classical mythology, such as Orion, the hunter son of the sea god Poseidon.

- **Norse myth says that the stars** were sparks that flew out of the fiery land of Muspelheim, set in the sky by the gods.

- **According to legend**, when Halley's Comet came speeding towards earth in 1835, a hero called Davy Crockett hurled it safely back into space.

- **An ancient myth from the Dogon people** of West Africa tells of a tiny planet that takes 50 years to orbit the star Sirius. It was not discovered by Western scientists until 1862.

- **In Greek mythology**, Antiope was the mother of the evening and morning star.

- **The Bororo tribe of South America believe** that the stars are naughty children who climbed into the heavens to escape punishment, but became trapped there.

■ **According to Inuit legend**, the Pleiades are a pack of hunting dogs that chased Nanook the Bear up into the sky.

■ **Astronomy was highly advanced** in the Toltec, Aztec, Inca and Maya civilizations. The Maya calendar did not just mark a yearly cycle of days and months, but tracked complicated patterns in time over three million years.

■ **In Native American mythology**, a hero called Poia, who grew up with the Blackfoot tribe, was the son of a star and a mortal woman.

■ **Some historians think** that the ancient Egyptians built their pyramids to launch the souls of their pharaohs to particular stars. For instance, the three pyramids at Giza line up with certain stars in the constellation Orion.

▶ *The three pyramids at Giza are one of the Seven Wonders of the Ancient World. The ancient Egyptians believed that the souls of pharaohs could reach the constellations from these great temples.*

Natural phenomena

■ **According to Greek myth**, winter occurs because the goddess of the harvest Demeter grieves for six months each year when her daughter Persephone has to live in the underworld.

■ **Hawaiian legends say** that the bad-tempered goddess Pele lives inside Mount Kilauea, spitting out lava to turn living things into stone.

■ **In Mayan mythology**, Kisin is an evil earthquake spirit. He lives under the earth with the souls of people who have killed themselves.

■ **Stories from Zambia and Zimbabwe** say that a shooting star is the storm god Leza watching over people.

■ **According to the Kono people** of Sierra Leone, the creator god once gave a bat a basket of darkness to look after. The bat spilled some, so it flies at night, trying to catch it.

■ **Some Native American myths** say that storms are created by an enormous flying creature with flashing eyes called the Thunderbird.

◄ *The phoenix was a magical bird that lived for 500 years without eating or drinking. Living in the deserts of the Middle East, when the time came for it to die, it set fire to itself. It was then reborn from the ashes.*

▲ *The glowing lights of the* Aurora Borealis *can sometimes be seen in the night skies over northern countries such as Norway, Sweden and Iceland.*

■ **In Chinese, the word dragon** also describes thunder and lightning. Tornadoes over oceans are known as sea dragons.

■ **In Norse myth**, the *Aurora Borealis*, or Northern Lights, are the glowing beauty of the frost giantess Gerda.

■ **Many ancient civilizations have myths** that feature firebirds, such as the phoenix. These may have arisen from the winged shape of light that blazes around the sun during a total eclipse.

■ **An Afro-Caribbean story** says that Anansi the spiderman accidentally smashed a pot containing all the common sense in the world. The wind spread it to all the creatures.

Animals and birds

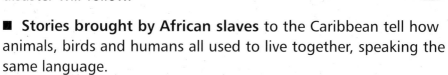

▶ The ancient Egyptians mummified cats and dogs, believing that if they preserved a dead body from decay, its spirit could live forever. Then they could be together in the afterlife.

■ **According to the Dogon of Africa**, animals once lived in heaven with the creator. Humans stole a male and a female of each animal by sliding them down the rainbow.

■ **Ravens have lived** at the Tower of London in England for over 1000 years. Myth says that if the birds ever leave, disaster will follow.

■ **Stories brought by African slaves** to the Caribbean tell how animals, birds and humans all used to live together, speaking the same language.

■ **Ancient Arab legends told** of an enormous bird called the roc. Modern scientists have since found the bones of a giant-sized bird in the swamps of Madagascar.

■ **In ancient Egypt**, cats were sacred to the goddess Bastet. When a pet cat died, the family had it mummified.

■ **The chief Norse god Odin** had two pet ravens, Hugin and Munin. They flew through the universe and brought back news.

■ **Around 600 BC**, a Greek slave called Aesop collected animal stories with a moral message. They have become known as *Aesop's Fables*.

■ **The Arikara tribe of Native Americans** believed that dogs were spirit messengers between them and their gods.

■ **Rudyard Kipling's *Just So* stories** (1902) are modern myths. They explain how animals came to be as they are – such as how the elephant got his trunk.

■ **The Greek goddess Athene** was often pictured with an owl on her shoulder. She was the goddess of intelligence, which is why owls have traditionally been thought of as wise birds.

▼ *Many legends have developed about dangerous wild creatures, such as the jaguar. Native Americans regarded the jaguar as a symbol of royalty and power.*

The Hare and the Tortoise

From *Aesop's Fables*

T he day that Tortoise challenged Hare
to a race, the animals laughed so
hard, their sides ached. But Tortoise
was fed up with Hare whizzing around him
all the time, teasing him about how slow he was. Hare made
Tortoise's head spin and left him feeling all of a fluster. "Poor old
plodder!" Hare would mock. "Silly old slowcoach!"

"I'll show that Hare, if it's the last thing I do!" Tortoise
promised himself. And before he realized what he was doing, he
bet Hare that he could beat him at running.

Hare thought that Tortoise's little joke was extremely funny.
For that's all Hare thought it was – a joke. Hare never expected
that Tortoise would actually go through with his mad idea. So
Hare's eyes nearly popped out of his head when, on the allotted
date and time, he arrived at the starting line to see Tortoise already
there, limbering up in a very slow, stiff, creaky sort of way.

"Be careful there, old chap," Hare said, as he realized his friend
was serious. "You don't want to do yourself an injury."

"Don't worry about me," replied Tortoise. "You should be
working out how you're going to beat me. Ha! You won't see me for
dust!" Tortoise had no idea how he was going to beat Hare – but he

wasn't going to let on. He was determined to do it somehow.

A huge crowd of animals gathered to watch the race. They all cheered and clapped, and jumped up and down with hilarity to see Tortoise throwing himself into his exercises and being cheeky to Hare.

Suddenly, Hare started to feel rather annoyed. "All right then. If that's the way you want it!" he snapped. "I was going to give you a headstart, but obviously you won't be wanting one."

"No need," breezed Tortoise, his heart pumping. "First one to the windmill's the winner."

Hare peered into the distance. He could get to the windmill in under a minute without even losing his breath. But surely it would take Tortoise all day to reach it!

There was no time for further discussion. The race was about to begin. "Three. Two. One. Go!" cried Barn Owl, and Tortoise lifted one leg over the starting line amid thunderous applause.

Stunned, Hare watched in amazement as Tortoise began to crawl slowly away. Well, you have to hand it to Tortoise. Hare thought, seeing the funny side of things again. He's certainly got a good sense of humour and a lot of guts!

Hare sat down next to the starting line under a shady tree. It was a beautiful sunny day and it was very pleasant to sit there in the dappled light, watching Tortoise amble peacefully into the first field. Hare's eyes shut and his head drooped before he even realized he was sleepy.

Meanwhile, Tortoise remembered what his dear old mum had told him as a child. Slow and steady does it, son. Tortoise kept on going. Keeping his eyes focused on the windmill, he tried to stop wondering what had happened to Hare. Slow and steady does it. Tortoise put his heart and soul into his running. He made up his mind. No matter what, he wouldn't give up.

Hare didn't wake up until the night air was so cold that it was freezing his whiskers. Where am I? he thought. And then suddenly he remembered the race. Leaping to his feet, he squinted into the moonlight, but there was no sign of Tortoise. All at once, he heard a faint sound of cheering coming from a long way off, and he saw tiny dark figures jumping up and down around the windmill. "Surely not!" Hare gasped, and shot off over the fields like an arrow. He arrived at the windmill just in time to see all the animals hoisting Tortoise – the champion – onto their shoulders. Tortoise looked red-faced and exhausted, but also delighted and proud, in a rather bashful way. Even Hare had to smile and offer to shake the winner's hand. After that, he never teased his friend about being slow again.

Moon mythology

◀ The moon god Thoth was also the god of writing, medicine and mathematics, and was the patron of the scribes. He was represented by the ibis (bird) because its beak was shaped like the crescent moon.

■ **In Inca mythology,** Mama Kilya, the moon goddess, was believed to be the mother of the Incas. Her husband, Inti the sun god, was the father of the Inca emperors.

■ **The moon god of the Inuit Native Americans** is called Igaluk. His sister Malina is the sun goddess.

■ **According to the Dakota Native Americans,** Hokewingla is a turtle spirit that lives in the moon.

■ **The moon god of magic and wisdom** is Thoth according to Egyptian myth. He is normally shown with an ibis (bird) as a head. Thoth controlled the Egyptian calendar.

■ **In Finnish mythology,** silver forms in the earth wherever light lands from the moon, Kuu.

■ **According to Chinese creation myth,** when Panku died his body formed the universe. His eyes became the sun and moon.

■ **The Greek goddess of the moon**, Selene, used magic to make a handsome shepherd called Endymion sleep forever, so she could enjoy his beauty for eternity.

■ **Sailors created myths** to pass on their knowledge of weather forecasting. One featured a mythical old mother, the moon, who lived in the sky. Mother Carey's chickens were storm petrels – seabirds that sailors believed could forecast storms.

■ **The Japanese moon god, Tsukiyomi**, once severely annoyed his sister the sun goddess, Amaterasu. This is why the sun and the moon never look each other in the face.

■ **The capital city of the Inca Empire**, Machu Picchu, lies up a mountain in the Andes in Peru. At the top of the neighbouring mountain, Huayna Picchu, is an Inca temple to the moon.

▶ *Masks were worn by Inuit shamans (magic healers) to portray spirits seen in dreams and visions. Carved from wood and decorated with feathers, this mask portrays Tarquq, the moon spirit.*

Magical creatures

■ **According to Chinese myth**, there were five types of dragon – dragons that guarded gods, dragons that guarded emperors, dragons that controlled wind and rain, dragons that deepened rivers and seas, and dragons that guarded hidden treasure.

■ **In Greek myth**, a centaur was half-man, half-horse. A satyr was half-man, half-goat.

■ **The phoenix** was a magical bird that lived for 500 years. It died by setting fire to itself, and was then born again from the ashes. J K Rowling features the phoenix throughout the *Harry Potter* series.

■ **Sleipnir was an eight-legged horse**, faster than the wind. He belonged to the chief Norse god Odin.

■ **In 1842 in America**, the famous Phineas T Barnum's travelling circus show displayed a 'real' mermaid. It turned out to be created from a monkey's body and a fish's tail!

▶ *Dragons are found in mythologies from all over the world, but play a particularly important role in traditional tales from China.*

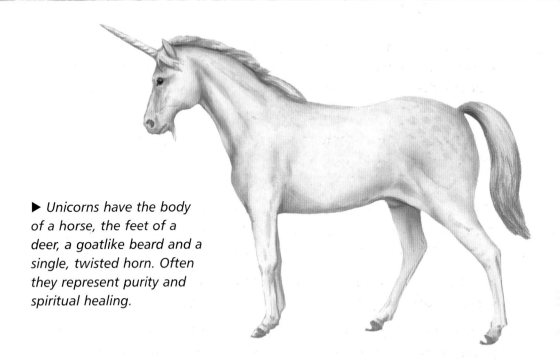

▶ *Unicorns have the body of a horse, the feet of a deer, a goatlike beard and a single, twisted horn. Often they represent purity and spiritual healing.*

■ **In the Caribbean**, mermaids are called water-mamas. People believe that if you get hold of a water-mama's comb, she will grant you a wish.

■ **Philippine myths tell of Alan** – creatures who are half-human, half-bird. They live in forests and look after children who have lost their parents.

■ **Unicorns are featured in the myths** of many civilizations. They are rare, beautiful creatures with the body of a horse and a twisted horn.

■ **In Chinese mythology**, Hsigo are monkeys with birdlike wings.

■ **Many Native American myths** involve the coyote, a trickster who is also tricked. The coyote is believed to possess human characteristics.

The Dragons of Peking

A Chinese folk tale

Once there was a poor prince who ruled over a group of peasants, living in a cluster of wooden huts in some dry, dusty fields. This sad little place was called Peking. However, the prince was good-hearted and determined, and had grand dreams of building Peking into a splendid city. The first thing he did was work hard with the men, women and children to build a high, solid wall with broad gates to keep enemies out.

The people were delighted. Little did they know that with all their digging, clearing, carrying and building, they'd disturbed two dragons who'd been asleep in an underground cave for thousands of years. You can imagine how grumpy the dragons felt when they were woken from their lovely long nap! "Who does this prince think he is," the first dragon growled, "getting his people to come banging around our cave like that!"

"Let's teach them all a lesson," the second dragon snorted.

That night, the two dragons wove a spell, turning themselves into an old man and an old woman. They stole away to the prince's house and, using magic, they crept past the royal guards, through several locked doors, into the very room where the prince lay, snoring soundly. The wrinkled couple asked, "O wise and gracious lord, we have come to ask your permission to leave your city of Peking and to take two baskets of water with us."

The prince stirred and murmured, "Why, of course you may," before falling back into a deep sleep.

The old man and woman hurried off to the river excitedly. It was narrow and muddy, but it was Peking's main source of water. They dipped their baskets into the stream and in minutes the river dwindled to a trickle, then dried up completely. Unbeknown to the prince, the disguised dragons' water baskets were enchanted – even if an entire ocean were poured into them, they would never be filled.

Next, the old man and woman took their water baskets, which were no heavier than before, off to the village spring. Soon, instead of a bubbling gush of water, there was just a muddy puddle. Then they visited every house in the village, draining all the water baskets of every last drop. Finally, the stooped pair hobbled off with their water baskets down the road that led out of Peking.

By the time the sun rose, the wicked old couple were far away.

Shouts of horror could be heard from all over Peking as the people woke and discovered that there was no water. Before long, there was a clamouring crowd outside the prince's house. "What shall we do?" they shouted. "Our lips are parched. We can't boil any rice for breakfast. Our crops are withering in the sun before our very eyes!"

A stale smell wafted under the prince's nostrils. "Oh dear," he sighed, "has anyone been able to have a bath this morning?" The people shuffled about and looked down, red-faced.

Then the prince remembered his dream about the two old people and their water baskets. Being a wise person who believed in magic, he was very suspicious and dashed off to see his faithful old advisor straight away.

"Aha!" his advisor nodded with a knowing smile. Mumbling under his breath, he took the prince straight off to the dragons' cave outside the city. When the faithful old advisor saw the cave was empty, he said, "Well, there you are then."

"Well, there I am then – what?" said the prince, rather frustrated.

"My father was told about this cave by his father, who was told by his father, who was told by his father, who was –"

"Yes, yes!" cried the prince impatiently. "Please get on with it!"

"Two dragons were asleep here, who obviously weren't very impressed with your plans to improve the city. They've taken your water and gone!"

At once the prince called for his spear and his horse, and shot down the road in a cloud of dust. He thundered past many travellers until, after hours of hard riding, he recognized the old couple from his dream and reined in his panting horse. "I gave my permission for an old man and woman to take two baskets of water," the prince yelled, "not the two dragons that you really are!" He plunged his spear into each of their baskets and water immediately began to gush out in a cascading torrent.

With a spine-chilling roar, the old couple began to change back into dragons before the prince's horrified eyes. But before the fire-breathing creatures could pounce on him, they were swept off in one direction by the swirling waters, while the prince on his horse was carried off in the other. All the surrounding countryside was submerged under water, and the prince's horse scrambled onto a jutting crag that poked up out of the water. It had once been the peak of a gigantic mountain.

"Now what am I to do?" frowned the prince, dripping from head to foot.

"I shall pray to heaven for help," came a voice. The prince looked round in surprise and saw a Buddhist monk, who had been sitting there so silently that the prince hadn't even noticed him. The monk shut his eyes and bowed his head ... and as he prayed – to the prince's enormous relief – the waters vanished. The prince thanked the Buddhist monk earnestly and began galloping back to Peking.

As soon as the prince neared the high, solid wall around his city, the people came pouring out of the gates with happy faces. "You'll never believe it!" they cried. "All our water has come back. But best of all, a brand new fountain has sprung up. It has swelled the river with water more sweet and crystal clear than any we have ever seen!"

Thanks to the magical fountain, the land around Peking changed from being a dry, dusty wasteland to a beautiful, lusciously green paradise. The prince fulfilled his plans of making the city one of the most splendid in the world and, as far as the people know, the dragons have never come back.

Holy people and prophets

- **Legend says that the founder of Sikhism**, Guru Nanak, once disappeared into a river. Days later he emerged, saying that he had been with god.

- **According to Greek myth**, the god Apollo condemned a woman called Cassandra to the fate of prophesying truthfully, but never being believed.

- **It is believed that** around AD 550, an Indian priest called Bodhidharma crossed the sea from China to Japan standing on a bamboo reed. He introduced Zen Buddhism to Japan.

- **The Druid High Priest, Cathbad**, was a great prophet in Celtic legend.

▼ *The Dome of the Rock is a mosque in Jerusalem built from AD 685–691 by an Arab caliph.*

▶ *The Japanese have traditionally loved creating beautiful gardens and parks, such as this rock garden. Zen Buddhist gardens are designed extremely simply to encourage serenity and meditation.*

■ **In 16th-century France**, Nostradamus wrote prophecies predicting world events as far ahead as AD 3500. Some people believe he foresaw the rise of Adolf Hitler and the death of Princess Diana.

■ **The earliest prophet of any world religion** was Zoroaster, who was born in northeast Persia (modern-day Iran) around 1200 BC.

■ **According to Greek myth**, a man called Tiresias was blinded by the gods, so they gave him the gift of prophecy as compensation.

■ **Mother Shipton was a prophetess** from North Yorkshire from the 16th century. Some people think she predicted the Great Fire of London, and the invention of railways, aircraft and the Internet.

■ **The Dome of the Rock in Jerusalem** was built on the spot, from which legend says, the prophet Muhammad ascended into heaven.

■ **Some people believe that** the great holy leaders in history, including Jesus, Krishna and the Buddha, have been manifestations of one great prophet – the Maitreya. According to the artist Benjamin Creme, the Maitreya is alive today and living in an Asian community in London, waiting for the right time to declare himself to the world.

Demons and devils

▲ *The Middle Eastern legend of Alaa U'Din, or Aladdin, tells how a poor boy finds a lamp containing a fearsome genie that can grant wishes.*

■ **The word devil comes from** the Hindu, *deva*; the word demon comes from the Greek, *daemon*; and the Christian word Satan comes from the Hebrew, *shatana*, meaning enemy.

■ **Some Nigerian tribes believe** that they can drive demons away by summoning up the spirits of their dead ancestors through masked dances.

■ **In Japanese myths**, Oni are demons with two horns, similar to devils in Christian stories. They wear tiger skins and fly around, hunting for the souls of evil people.

■ **In myths from the Middle East**, fiery demons are often known as *djin*. These came to be known in Western myths as genies.

■ **Demons in Hindu mythology** may have been inspired by the people who lived in India, before the ancestors of the Hindus invaded.

▲ *The curved roof of the Temple of Confucius is designed according to traditional Chinese beliefs to ward off demons. Confucius was a Chinese leader who lived from 551–479 BC. Millions of people still follow his teachings today.*

■ **Gargoyles are carved stone demons** that drain water from church roofs. The name comes from a great dragon, Gargouille, who was believed to live in the river Seine, Paris.

■ **The Christian image of the devil** probably came from pictures of the Greek nature god, Pan. Pan was half-man, half-goat, with cloven hooves and two horns.

■ **The roofs of Chinese temples** were built curving upwards at the edges so that any demons falling from the sky would be swept up and away.

■ **The evil Hindu demon, Ravana**, had ten heads and twenty arms. He tricked the god of creation into giving him special powers of protection, so he couldn't be harmed by gods or other demons.

■ **In Sumerian myth**, a dreaded female demon is known as Lamashtu, which means 'she who destroys'.

Giants

◀ *The 19th-century writer Oscar Wilde wrote the famous story,* The Selfish Giant, *in which a giant befriends a mysterious little boy, who teaches him how to be happy.*

■ **The ancient Greeks believed** that the immortals Gaea and Uranus gave birth to three 100-handed giants called the Hecatoncheires, and three one-eyed giants called the Cyclopes.

■ **In Celtic legend**, the Fomorian giant, Balor, had an evil eye. One glance killed whoever it fell upon.

■ **In Norse mythology**, the giants were the sworn enemies of the gods. Their ruler was King Utgard-Loki.

■ **Several passages from the Old Testament** of the Bible tell of tribes and kingdoms of giant-sized people.

■ **The most famous giant** in the Bible was the warrior Goliath, killed by the shepherd boy David.

■ **According to the Mesopotamian** epic poem *Gilgamesh*, the home of the gods in the Cedar Forest of Lebanon was guarded by a ferocious giant called Humbaba.

■ **A giant man** holding a club is carved into the hillside at Cerne Abbas in Dorset, England. No one knows who made him or why. Historians think he may date from AD 185.

■ **In Greek myth**, Talos was a fearsome giant made of bronze who guarded the island of Crete.

■ **Big, stupid, clumsy, and greedy giants** feature in myths and legends from many parts of the world. In some stories, they represent the forces of nature, such as earthquakes or thunder. In others, they embody feelings of rage or jealousy.

■ **Many modern myths and legends** also include giants. J K Rowling's *Harry Potter* series features a friendly half-giant, Rubeus Hagrid, who is a teacher at Hogwarts School of Witchcraft and Wizardry.

▼ *According to the legends of European settlers in North America, the Grand Canyon was formed when a giant lumberjack called Paul Bunyan walked along trailing his pickaxe on the ground behind him.*

David and Goliath

From the Old Testament of the Bible

L ong, long ago, in the days when prophets walked in the holy land and the Lord God spoke to the people, there lived in Israel a shepherd boy named David. He was the youngest in his family, and very precious to his father because his three elder brothers had all enlisted in King Saul's army and were fighting in a war against the Philistines. David's father did not know whether he would see his three eldest sons alive again. He worried about them dreadfully and his eyes always looked dull and tired. One day, David noticed his father packing some grain, bread and cheese. "Take these things to your brothers, David," he urged his youngest son. "Then hurry home and tell me how they are doing. Send them our love."

When David reached the battlefield, the soldiers were retreating in a panic, running from the front line as fast as they could. David couldn't believe his eyes and was nearly trampled on. Then he saw the enemy, and he understood.

On the far side of the battlefield, standing alone, was the biggest man David had ever seen. As tall as two men, he had colossal legs like huge tree trunks, and a booming voice that shook the trees. Grasping a spear the size of a battering ram, the giant's mighty body was clad in enormous bronze armour. "Who is that?" David gasped, rooted to the spot.

The soldiers nearby explained. "It's Goliath of Gath," they told David. "Each time we're ready to attack, he strides out and challenges us to settle things by a duel. He says that if any Israelite can beat him, then the Philistines will be our slaves. But if he beats our soldier, then the Philistines will take all of us into slavery. The king has offered a huge reward to anyone who'll fight him, including his daughter's hand in marriage. But who could beat such a giant?"

"I'd give anything for the chance!" shouted David defiantly, and he went to find the king.

At first, King Saul was reluctant to let the young shepherd boy face the huge warrior. But there was something about the way David spoke that conviniced the king he might not be sending the boy to his death. "God has given me the strength to fight bears when I am looking after my father's sheep," David said, "and now I know he'll give me the strength to beat this giant!" So Saul gave David permisson to try.

The king dressed the shepherd boy in his own royal armour for the fight, but David wasn't very big and it totally swamped him. He could hardly stand, let alone walk. And the weight of Saul's hefty sword and shield made his arms ache. So David took off all the equipment, until he stood there in his simple shepherd's robe, holding only his sling, his crook and a small cloth bag of five smooth, round stones.

When Goliath saw the tiny figure coming out to meet him, he threw back his head and laughed. "Am I a dog, that you come with a stick to beat me?" he boomed, mockingly. "Come on then, a little closer!" he taunted.

"I'll mince you into little pieces and then feed you to the wild beasts."

David was completely unruffled by the gigantic warrior. "You may have mighty weapons, but I'm armed with the most mighty weapon of them all, the name of the Lord God of Israel. It's you who will be fed to the birds and wild beasts, not me!"

At these cheeky words, Goliath gave a mighty roar and strode forwards. David reached into his bag for a stone, took aim and slung it. The little pebble hit the centre of the giant's forehead, sinking into him. Without even realizing what had hit him, Goliath keeled over like a felled tree and crumpled into the dust. David ran up to the massive body, took Goliath's own huge sword, and chopped off Goliath's head.

On the far side of the battlefield, a stunned silence descended over the Philistine army. David, the brave shepherd boy, was a hero. Not only had he done the unthinkable and defeated the mighty giant, he had won the war. The jubilant Israelites charged, forcing the Philistines to run for their lives, all the way back to their cities.

Witches and wizards

■ **Stories from eastern Europe** tell of a wicked witch called Baba Yaga with sharp teeth made of iron. She lives in the forest in a house that scuttles about on hens' legs.

■ **The magician Merlin** was King Arthur's most trusted advisor. Merlin warned Arthur that Guinevere would bring him grief – and indeed she did.

■ **Sikkim is a tiny kingdom** in the Himalayas where belief in magic is still strong. A maharaja who died in 1963, Sir Tashi Namgyal, was believed to be able to control the weather.

■ **Greeks and Romans worshipped** the goddess of darkness, Hecate. She is seen as a symbol of horror and is often associated with black magic.

■ **Entertainers on the Indonesian island** of Bali perform myths about a witch called Rangda. The character came from a wicked queen called Mahendradatta who lived 1000 years ago.

■ **Aztec sorcerers used black mirrors** of polished obsidian to predict the future. Their patron was the god Tezcatlipoca, which means lord of the smoking mirror.

▶ *Well known for being the companions of witches and wizards, black cats are mysterious creatures, often depicted lurking in the shadows. Some people believe that cats could even cast spells.*

▶ *One of Shakespeare's most famous tragedies is* Macbeth. *Set in Scotland, Macbeth, one of King Duncan's generals, kills Duncan to become king himself. The play opens with three witches who foretell that Macbeth will become the king.*

■ **In 1487, James Sprenger and Henry Kramer wrote** *The Malleus Maleficarum* – a book of rules for detecting witches. It was used by the church in Europe for 300 years to accuse people of black magic and condemn them to death.

■ **One of the most famous wizards** is Gandalf, a character in J R R Tolkien's *The Lord of the Rings* stories. A wise and powerful wizard, Gandalf fights the evil of the Dark Lord Sauron.

■ **In the days of Queen Elizabeth I**, all the witches in Hampshire gathered to create a 'cone of power' to chase the Spanish Armada away from England. In fact, a severe storm drove the fleet back to Spain and few ships arrived intact.

■ **In Greek mythology**, an enchantress called Circe knew very powerful magic. Once, she changed Odysseus and his men into pigs as punishment for landing on her island.

Baba Yaga, the Bony-legged Witch

A Russian folk tale

There was once a wicked woman who hated her stepdaughter so much that she pushed the little girl out of the house and told her to go and borrow a needle and thread from Baba Yaga, the bony-legged witch. The girl's father was at work, so she had no one to turn to and she was terrified. Baba Yaga, the bony-legged witch, lived in the middle of the deep, dark forest, in a hut that moved about on hens' legs. Nevertheless, the little girl dared not disobey her cruel stepmother, so off she went into the depths of the dim forest, alone and very frightened.

The little girl was soon among tall, prickly trees that whispered all around her, and she quite forgot which way was which. Tears began to glisten in her eyes and slowly roll down her flushed cheeks.

"Do not weep, little girl," came a cheerful voice. The little girl looked up to see that a nightingale was talking to her. "You are a kind-hearted girl and I will tell you what I can to help you. Along the path, you will come across some objects. Pick them up and make sure you use them wisely."

So the girl set off again, further into the gloomy forest. As she walked along, she saw a neatly folded handkerchief lying among the pine needles, and she put it in her pocket. A little further on, she spied some ribbons that were dangling from the branches. She took those and slipped them into her pocket, too. A few steps on, she spotted a little can of oil, laying amongst some rocks. She picked up the oil can and placed it with the other things. Next, she came across a large bone and a maple leaf sprinkled with some juicy morsels of meat – and then her pocket was full.

It wasn't long before some big iron gates came into view up ahead, and beyond them was the hut of Baba Yaga running about on its hens' legs. The little girl shivered with fear. Suddenly, a howling wind rose up, sending the branches of the trees whipping fiercely around her head. "I'll never get near that horrible hut at this rate," the little girl sighed, ducking the boughs coming at her thick and fast. Then she remembered the things she had collected along the way. Pulling out the ribbons from her pocket, she tied them carefully onto the trees. As soon as she did, the wind dropped to a gentle breeze and the branches became still.

Then the little girl tried to push open the gates, but a dreadful creaking and groaning tore through the air. She took the oil can from her pocket and covered the hinges with oil. After that, the gate opened without a squeak, and the girl passed through.

All of a sudden, a drooling, snarling dog came running at her out of nowhere, barking ferociously. Quick as a flash, the girl threw the big, juicy bone to the dog. He forgot his attack immediately and lay down to gnaw at his unexpected treat.

Now the only obstacle left to face was the hut itself, scuttling about on its awful scaly legs. And there, standing in the shadows, was the ugliest woman the girl had ever seen – a thin, bony figure with dark, shining eyes and long, green hair. It had to be Baba Yaga, the bony-legged witch!

"Come in, my dear," grinned the witch, showing her sharp, iron teeth. "While I'm searching for that needle and thread you want, you can have a nice bath and do my spinning for me." Baba Yaga gripped the girl's arm with her clawlike fingers and pulled her into the house. "Run her a bath and be quick!" she screamed at her pale-faced maid, before whispering, "Make sure you scrub her well, all ready for eating." With a wry smile, Baba Yaga swept from the room, leaving the girl and the maid alone.

The pale-faced maid began to bustle about, filling the bath with water, and fetching soap and a hard, dirty scrubbing brush. The little girl saw that she was trembling with fear.

"I am sorry that you have to live and work here," the little girl said. "Here, have this handkerchief as a little present to cheer you up."

"Oh, thank you," the maid sighed, gazing in delight at beautiful silky red handkerchief. "I will use a teacup instead of a jug to fill the bath, so you have more time to escape."

Then the little girl noticed a skinny black cat cowering in the corner. "You don't look as if you've eaten properly for ages," she said, stroking his tatty fur. "Here, have these scraps of meat."

"Oh, thank you," the skinny black cat purred, washing his paws. "I will do the spinning for you, so you have more time to escape. Now take this magic towel and comb, and run for your life. When you hear Baba Yaga coming, throw each of them behind you, one by one. Be quick and go right away."

So the girl took the magic towel and comb, and ran as quickly as she could into the shadows of the towering trees. Back at the hut, the cat sat at the spinning wheel, tangled the wool into a ball to hide behind, and began to spin.

Several times, the witch passed the open door of the room and peered in. But when she heard the whirr of the spinning wheel and saw the pile of tangled wool, she went away, content. But by and by, the witch began to get suspicious that the pile of wool wasn't getting smaller. "Are you sure you know how to spin properly?" she screeched.

"Yes," yowled the cat, trying to sound like the girl but failing.

Baba Yaga realized she had been tricked. She screamed with fury, her face turning scarlet. Rushing into the room, she grabbed the cat by the scruff of the neck. "Why did you let the girl escape?" she howled.

"You've never given me anything but leftovers," the cat hissed. "That kind girl gave me tasty morsels of meat."

Furious, Baba Yaga stalked over to the pale-faced maid and slapped her. "Why did you let the girl escape?" she growled.

"You've never given me a single present," the pale-faced maid shouted. "That kind girl gave me a lovely hanky."

Storming outside, Baba Yaga kicked the dog who was happily chomping on his bone. "Why did you let the girl escape?"

"You've never given me a bone or a treat," the dog barked. "That kind girl gave me a big, juicy bone to chew on."

With incredible force, Baba Yaga kicked the iron gates. "Why did you let the girl escape?" she shouted.

"You let us get all stiff and rusty," they creaked. "That kind girl soothed our aching joints with lashings of lovely oil."

Finally, Baba Yaga threatened the birch trees with an axe. "Why did you let the girl escape?" she howled.

"You've never once decorated our branches," they roared, "but that kind girl dressed us with beautiful ribbons."

Gnashing her iron teeth wildly, she jumped on her broomstick and raced off through the deep, dark forest after the little girl. Hearing the swish of the air, the little girl knew the witch was coming and so threw down the magic towel. Suddenly, a wide rushing river appeared before Baba Yaga, soaking her broomstick so badly that it could no longer fly. Spitting and cursing, Baba Yaga had to leave her broomstick and slowly wade across the river. Once she was free of the water, she began to run after the little girl.

Hearing the pounding of Baba Yaga's footsteps, the little girl knew the witch was coming, and so threw down the magic comb. All of a sudden, a rainforest sprang up in front of Baba Yaga, so thick and tangled that Baba Yaga could do nothing to find her way through it. Squawking and screaming, and gnashing her iron teeth, she stormed back to her dreary hut, shouting all the way.

With her home in sight, the little girl heaved a sigh of relief, especially when standing at the door of her house was her beloved father. She rushed to tell him all about her stepmother's evil plot, without leaving out any details. Her father was horrified. He sent the wicked woman out of the house at once and drove her into the magic rainforest. From that day to this, she has never been seen again.

Whatever became of her, the little girl and her father lived happily on their own, and pleased with her generosity and thoughtful nature, the nightingale came to visit every day.

Mothers and matriarchies

▲ *According to the Greek poet, Hesiod, the goddess Aphrodite was born from foam on the sea. One legend says that waves carried her to shore at Paphos in Cyprus.*

■ **Many mythologies** come from male-ruled societies, or patriarchies. However, earlier cultures – usually farming tribes – lived in female-ruled societies, or matriarchies.

■ **Matriarchies grew from** the importance of mother earth in producing food, and of human mothers in producing children.

■ **Mother earth is the creator goddess**, representing everything in nature. She has different names in different cultures.

■ **In many matriarchies**, an honoured young man became the queen's sacred king for a year. At the end of this time, he was sacrificed to their great goddess for a plentiful harvest.

■ **The great goddesses of ancient Greece**, including Gaea, Athene, Hera, Artemis and Aphrodite, became less important when male-dominated myths about Zeus took over.

■ **The Aztecs had a terrifying mother earth goddess** called Coatlicue who could only be satisfied by human sacrifice.

■ **Celtic mothers-to-be** used to pray for help in childbirth to the goddess Frigg, Odin's wife.

■ **In Greek myth**, the hero Oedipus grew up without knowing his parents. A prophecy said that he would one day unknowingly marry his own mother – and he did.

■ **Many Christian stories** tell how the mother of Jesus has appeared throughout history in visions to young people, such as to Saint Bernadette at Lourdes.

■ **The Hopi, Hokohan and Zuni** Native American tribes lived in a matriarchal society. However, their religious ceremonies were mostly held by men, wearing masks to represent nature spirits.

Fertility mythology

■ **Farmer's wives in** ancient Greece often set an extra place at the table hoping that the goddess of the harvest, Demeter, would bless them by joining them at their meal.

■ **Each April, the Aztecs smeared** reeds with their blood and offered them to Cinteotl, the god of maize, to ensure a good food supply.

■ **The Japanese goddess** of fertility and nourishment for all life was called Uke-Mochi-No-Kami.

▼ *Njord is the Norse god of the sea and the fertility of the coast. He leads the Vanir, the fertility gods, and although he is married to the goddess Skadi, they live separately – Njord over the sea and Skadi in the forests.*

▶ *Sobek was the ancient Egyptian god of the river Nile, and thus of the fertility of the land.*

■ **An Iroquois Native American myth** tells how the corn goddess, Onatah, was kidnapped by the ruler of the underworld. During the time her mother searched for her, no crops grew. This tale is similar to a Greek myth about the goddess Demeter and her daughter Persephone.

■ **In Egyptian mythology**, the fertility goddess Hathor was represented as a cow.

■ **According to Slavic legend**, Simargl was a creature like a winged dog. He was responsible for scattering the seeds of every plant across the world.

■ **In Sumerian mythology**, Tammuz was god of agriculture. He died each year and was brought back from the underworld by Ishtar, the goddess of love and war.

■ **The Incas often sacrificed** llamas to the fertility goddess, Pachamama.

■ **In ancient Indian mythology**, the god Indra fights a dragon of drought and releases seven rivers to make the earth fertile again.

■ **Baal was an important fertility god** who was widely worshipped by ancient peoples in the Middle East.

Old age and long life

■ **In classical myth**, the prophetess, the Sibyl, wished to live for 1000 years, but did not ask for eternal youth. She gradually aged and shrunk until she had to live in a bottle.

■ **In another classical myth**, the goddess, Eos, asked Zeus to make Tithonus immortal. Tithonus became a withered old man forever as she also forgot to ask for eternal youth.

■ **In the traditional fairy tale**, *Sleeping Beauty*, when the princess pricks her finger and falls asleep, the whole kingdom sleeps, too. Although she does not wake up for 100 years, she does not age at all.

■ **A Norse story** tells how a wrinkled old woman called Elli once wrestled the great god Thor to one knee. Elli was old age in disguise – and old age defeats everyone in the end.

▶ *Genies are often depicted as magical spirits who grant wishes to their master. The genie of the lamp in* Aladdin *is trapped for eternity in the lamp until Aladdin sets him free.*

▶ *The American writer Washington Irving wrote the story* Rip Van Winkle *based on a Dutch legend. The main character, Rip, falls asleep in a dwarf cavern and wakes up to find that he is 20 years older.*

■ **The Chinese god**, Shou Lao, decides how long a person will live. He is often pictured with a turtle or a white crane – symbols of long life.

■ **In Japanese mythology**, tortoises and storks often symbolize old age.

■ **In Celtic legend**, the goddess Niamh carried away an Irish prince called Oisin to the land of youth, Tir Nan Og. When Oisin returned home, he had been away for 300 years!

■ **In Celtic myth**, Lir was the old man of the sea. His second wife secretly turned his children into swans and drove them away. By the time Lir found them and reversed the spell, they had become old people themselves.

■ **According to the Bible**, in the early days of the world, people lived for a long time. Noah lived for 950 years.

■ **The story of *Peter Pan*** by James Barrie tells of a boy who never grows up. He lives for eternity in Neverland as a child, having many adventures with his friends, the Lost Boys and Wendy.

Rip Van Winkle

An American legend

In a village in the foothills of the Catskill Mountains of
America lived a man called Rip Van Winkle. Everybody liked
Rip. He was a generous, easy-going man who was always glad
to lend a hand to his neighbours. In fact, Rip Van Winkle was
always doing anybody else's work – except his own. His wife
nagged him about it all day long! "Rip, if you're not too busy
varnishing Mrs Green's fence, you can mend the holes in the shed
… Instead of helping to burn the farmer's rubbish, you can feed
the chickens and milk the cows … Then if you can stop yourself
from building Arne Jacob's wall for him, there's our potatoes to
dig up, and the wagon to be washed down, and the gutters to be
cleared out, and the yard to be swept and …" And so it was every
day, on and on.

Every now and again, Rip Van Winkle whistled for his faithful dog, Wolf, shouldered his gun, and strode away from his wife without a word. Off he would stroll up the mountainside, along the river and through the pine forests until his wife's screeching voice had faded away. The only sounds were birdsong, the rustling of the trees, and the panting of Wolf by his side. Rip knew there would be trouble when he got home, but a day off in the peaceful sunshine was well worth it.

One day when Rip had disappeared on one of these rambles, he was taking a rest under a shady tree, when he heard a voice calling his name. "Rip Van Winkle! Rip Van Winkle!" came the high, shrill cry.

Wolf's ears flattened against his skull and he gave a long, low growl. Rip looked in the direction Wolf was snarling and there among the long grass was a bearded man no higher than his own boot, struggling under the weight of a big beer barrel.

"Rip Van Winkle!" shouted the dwarf, crossly. "Will you give me a hand with this barrel before it squashes me!"

Rip was so used to doing what he was told that he jumped up to help at once.

"That's better," wheezed the dwarf, as Rip took one end of the heavy barrel. "Now up we go!" Rip lurched forwards as the dwarf stomped away up the mountain.

After at least an hour's tramping and much huffing and puffing, the dwarf led Rip Van Winkle straight behind a thundering waterfall, through a hidden door and into an enormous cavern.

Dwarves were everywhere. Some were dressed in aprons, pouring endless tankards of beer out of big kegs just like the one Rip was helping to carry. Others were playing nine pins, rolling smooth round black rocks at copper skittles, and cheering loudly. Yet more dwarves were drinking and clinking their tankards together, singing songs.

"Pull up a chair," Rip's new friend invited him, lowering the barrel to the floor and passing him a tankard. "Help yourself to a drink. You must be thirsty after that climb – I know I am!"

The stunned Rip Van Winkle did just that. "My, that's mighty powerful stuff!" he spluttered, as he swallowed down a huge gulp of the dwarf beer. "But whatever it is, it's very good!" he licked his lips and poured himself another. The dwarves didn't take a blind bit of notice of him, so Rip Van Winkle sat back and began to watch the nine pins competition. "Well, this is a most pleasant way to spend the afternoon," he thought, helping himself to another beer … and another. And before Rip Van Winkle even realized he was drunk, he had slumped onto a huge flat rock and was snoring loudly.

When Rip woke up, the cavern was empty. "Come on, Wolf," he yawned, and they both stood up and stretched. "We'd better hurry back or we'll never hear the last of it." So with a heavy heart, they strode through the little door, out from behind the waterfall and off down the mountain. "Wait for it," he murmured to his dog as he climbed the porch steps to his house. "Any minute now, that wife of mine will start screeching fit to wake the dead." Rip put his hand on the doorknob and turned, but it failed to open. "Well, this needs a bit of oil," he murmured to himself. He rattled the knob and twisted it about. "Funny," Rip remarked, "I think it's locked. She never locks the door, never."

At that very moment, the front door opened and there stood a woman with an angry face. "Who are you?" the woman snapped. "What are you up to, trying to get in my front door?" Rip Van Winkle had never seen her before.

"Who are you?" gasped Rip. "What are you doing in my house?"

"Your house!" the woman scoffed. "I've lived here for over nineteen years, thank you very much!"

Rip Van Winkle backed off the porch and looked around him. He scratched his head and stared. The woman was right – it wasn't his house. Well, it looked similar to his house, but the curtains at the window were different. There were strange chairs on the verandah, and plants that he had never seen before. The wagon in the yard was not his wagon.

"But – I – How –" stuttered Rip. "Where's Mrs Van Winkle?"

"Mrs Van Winkle?" the puzzled woman gawped. "She left here nearly twenty years ago, just after her husband wandered off and disappeared. Now, be off with you or I'll call the police!"

"Twenty years!" marvelled Rip Van Winkle, as he staggered away, stroking his beard. His beard! Suddenly Rip realized that his beard hung down to his knees. The woman's words had to be true! He had been asleep for twenty years!

Rip Van Winkle's hands trembled with the shock as he reached down and patted the bemused Wolf comfortingly. Then his mouth began to curve upwards in a small smile. "Just imagine, Wolf," he murmured. "No more nagging – ever!" With that, he turned and strode across the street, whistling a merry tune. Fortunately, the inn was in the same place as it always had been – and when the townspeople heard his story, he never had to buy himself another pint of beer again.

Learning and knowledge

■ **According to Norse myth**, the chief warrior god, Odin, bought a drink from the fountain of knowledge at the foot of the world tree. The price was one of his own eyes.

■ **Ancient Egyptians believed** that the god of wisdom, Thoth, devised laws, worked out how to measure time, and invented hieroglyphic writing.

▼ The ancient Egyptians believed that hieroglyphic writing came from the god Thoth. Only priests and scribes knew how to write, and they would pray to Thoth for success in their work.

▶ *Early Greek coins carried the symbol of the goddess of wisdom, Athene – an owl.*

■ **The Celtic goddess** of learning was called Brigid, meaning the powerful one.

■ **According to Inca legend**, the creator god Viraccocha roamed the world to teach wisdom to humankind. However, people were too busy with crime and war to listen.

■ **In Chinese myth**, Guan Di is the wise god of law, martial arts and diplomacy. Although born as a mortal, he became such a courageous warrior that he was made a god.

■ **Japanese people believed** that it was their god of learning, Tenjin, who taught them how to write.

■ **In Tibetan Buddhism**, eight giant warriors called Dharmapalas have the power to scorch enemies of truth with the light of perfect knowledge.

■ **The Hindu god** of learning is Hanuman, who is half-human, half-monkey. He was taught his immense knowledge by the god Surya.

■ **According to Muslim Shia stories**, teachers called Sayyids are direct descendants of the Prophet Muhammad. They are gifted with learning from birth.

■ **Athene is the Greek goddess of war** and wisdom. In many myths, she teaches and helps heroes, such as Bellerophon, in their deeds.

Legendary partnerships

■ **The Norse gods Thor** and Loki once partnered up to win back Thor's magic hammer from a giant who had stolen it. They went to the giant's castle disguised as a bride and bridesmaid.

■ **A partnership formed between a Greek monster** called Scylla and a whirlpool called Charybis. If sailors attempted to avoid one of the monsters, they were immediately in danger of the other.

▼ *Legend says that the outlaw Robin Hood and his band of Merry Men lived in Sherwood Forest, near Nottingham in England. They robbed from the rich to give to the poor.*

■ **English legends** about a hero called Robin Hood have been told since the 14th century. He teamed up with a gang of Merry Men. They had many adventures, stealing from their enemy, the Sheriff of Nottingham.

■ **According to the Fon people of Africa**, the world remains fertile due to the partnership of Sagbata, god of the earth, and Sogbo, god of the sky. Sagbata gives Sogbo control of the earth and all living things, as long as Sogbo sends down life-giving rain.

■ **In Greek myth**, Jason takes a group of heroes called the Argonauts on his quest to find the Golden Fleece.

■ **The Knights of the Round Table** were the bravest heroes of medieval times. In one tale, Sir Tristram battles and kills a giant and a dragon, proving his worth and courage.

■ **Twin brothers Romulus and Remus** were believed to have founded Rome. After disagreeing about who should be the emperor, Romulus killed Remus.

■ **Sir Arthur Conan Doyle** first published stories about Sherlock Holmes in the late 19th century. The great detective was accompanied in his investigations by Dr Watson, who was also the narrator of the tales.

■ **In J K Rowling's *Harry Potter* series**, Hermione and Ron are Harry's friends at Hogwarts. They help him to defeat his archenemy, Voldemort.

■ ***The Wonderful Wizard of Oz*** is a tale about Dorothy, Lion, Tinman and Scarecrow. They travel together to Oz to find the wizard, as only he can help them with their individual needs. Lion wants courage, Tinman needs a heart, Scarecrow doesn't have a brain, and Dorothy wants to go home.

The Thunder God Gets Married

A Norse myth

Up in heaven, Thor the thunder god was furious. Someone had stolen his magic hammer – the terror of the gods. Whenever he threw it, it killed anything in its path, then always returned to his hand. It was the gods' most deadly weapon against their enemies, the giants.

Now the raging Thor's roaring sounded like clouds clashing together. His black face sent a dark shadow over the whole sky. As Thor hurled blazing lightning bolts through the clouds, the troublemaker god, Loki, came nervously to see him. "I have good news, my friend," Loki explained. "I have found out that it is the giant Thrym who has stolen your hammer. He has agreed to give it back on one condition – that he has the most beautiful of all the goddesses, Freya, as his bride."

The thunder god's sulky face brightened a little and he charged off to find Freya. "Put on your best frock, Freya!" Thor boomed, throwing open her wardrobe doors. "You have to marry the giant Thrym so I can get my magic hammer back."

Freya's eyes flickered with cold fire. "Excuse me, Thor," she said, calmly. "Would you care to repeat that?"

"You-have-to-marry-the-giant-Thrym-so-I-can-get-my-magic-hammer-back!" the impatient thunder god cried at top speed.

Glaring, Freya stood with her hands on her hips. "Firstly, Thor, I don't have to *do* anything."

Thor's face reddened.

"Secondly," Freya continued, "I wouldn't marry that ugly monster Thrym if he were the only creature left in the world."

Ashamed, the thunder god hung his head.

"Thirdly," Freya finished, "it's your problem, you sort it out."

"Sorry, Freya," Thor mumbled, shuffling about a bit. Then he turned and stormed back to Loki. The two gods sat down glumly and wracked their brains to come up with another way to get the hammer.

"How about …" Thor started to suggest. Then he shook his head. "No, no good."

"What if …" Loki began, his eyes brightening. Then his face fell. "No, it would never work."

It looked as if Thor's magic hammer would have to stay in the land of the giants forever – until the god Heimdall had an idea …

"That's absolutely out of the question!" Thor thundered.

"Outrageous!" Loki squealed. "I'll never do it!"

"Well, you come up with another plan then," Heimdell laughed, knowing that there wasn't one.

That night, the giant Thrym was delighted to see a chariot carrying his future bride and her bridesmaid rumbling up to his castle steps. "It's Freya!" the gormless giant gasped with delight. He commanded a magnificent wedding banquet to be prepared at once.

Thrym was far too excited to notice how big and clumsy the bride and bridesmaid looked in their frilly dresses. Thrym didn't take in that the women had low, gruff voices and huge, hairy hands. And he hardly thought twice about the way that Freya swigged down two whole barrels of beer and devoured an entire roast ox.

When all the guests had eaten and drunk their fill, the beaming Thrym got to his feet to make a speech. "My wife and I," he began, blushing, "would like to thank you all for coming here today. Freya has made me the luckiest being in the whole universe. And now, I will keep my word and give back the magic hammer I stole from that ugly thug of a thunder god."

A roll of drums sounded as one of Thrym's servants brought in the magic hammer on a cushion. Thrym held it high in the air for his marvelling guests to admire, then with a grand flourish, he presented it to his bride.

"The ugly thug of a thunder god thanks you!" roared Thor, ripping off his veil and springing to his feet. And before Thrym and his guests could really take in the trick, they were lying dead on the floor and the wedding feast was unexpectedly over.

All the gods were truly relieved to have the magic hammer back in Thor's hands, where it belonged. But it was a long time before Thor and Loki could laugh with the other gods about how charming they both looked in a dress!

Tales of beauty

◀ *The statue Venus de Milo is around 2100 years old. She was found on the island of Milos in the Aegean Sea during the 2nd century* BC. *Today the statue is found in the Louvre art gallery and museum in Paris, France.*

■ **In Greek myth, the goddesses Hera, Athene and Aphrodite** wanted to know who was the most beautiful. The chief god Zeus asked a Trojan prince called Paris to decide. Paris picked Aphrodite because she promised him the most beautiful woman in the world.

■ **According to Greek myth**, Aphrodite was the goddess of beauty and love. At birth, she emerged from the sea fully grown, and the winds blew her ashore.

■ **The Romans adopted Aphrodite** under the name of Venus. She was also the official protector of the Roman people.

■ **Classical myth says** that the most beautiful woman in the world was Queen Helen of Sparta – the daughter of Zeus and the goddess Nemesis.

■ **Paris seized Helen as his reward** and stole her away to Troy. This action caused the start of the Trojan Wars.

■ **In Hindu myth,** Lakshmi was the goddess of beauty and good fortune.

■ **The Norse goddess of beauty** Freya drove a chariot pulled by two large cats. She was once given the Brising Necklace by the black dwarves. The necklace was cursed and Freya was tricked into marrying the dwarves.

■ **The Celts had a god** of beauty and love – Angus Og.

■ **A Celtic story says that the wizard Math** made the hero Llew Llaw Gyffesa a beautiful wife out of blossoms. She was named Blodeuwedd, or flower face.

■ **The legend of *Beauty and the Beast*** was first recorded by the French writer Madame Gabrielle de Villeneuve, in 1740. In 1756, Madame Le Prince de Beaumont rewrote it into the version most people know today.

▶ *In Greek mythology, sea sirens, or nymphs, were beautiful women who sang enchanting songs to lure sailors closer to the rocks. This caused their boats to crash and the sailors to drown.*

Living happily ever after

■ **In Greek myth, Penelope was the wife** of the hero Odysseus. She waited for 20 years for her husband to return from the Trojan Wars.

■ **The Japanese goddess of love** Benten once set out to get rid of the evil Serpent King. However, the couple fell in love. The Serpent King promised to change his ways and they were married.

■ **According to one Robin Hood myth**, the folk hero rescued Maid Marian from the advances of King John I and married her himself.

■ **A Chinese myth tells** how a servant once disguised himself as a magical rainbow-coloured dog and won the emperor's permission to marry his daughter.

■ **The Greek hero Perseus rescued Andromeda** from being sacrificed to a sea monster. Their names live on today as constellations.

▶ *The Buddha taught that people should aim to achieve absolute peace – a state called nirvana.*

▶ Celtic prophecy said that a girl called Deirdre would bring ruin on Ireland, so she was locked away in a castle, yearning for freedom and her love, the king's nephew.

■ **There are many Japanese myths** in which devoted, faithful lovers are turned into pine trees. Pine trees symbolize fidelity in marriage.

■ **According to Roman myth**, Psyche was a girl who boasted that she was more beautiful than the goddess Venus. The god Cupid was sent to punish Psyche, but instead he fell in love with her. They ran away together and Psyche was finally made a goddess.

■ **In the Scottish legend Tam Lin**, a brave girl wins a man captured by the Queen of Fairies by holding him tightly while the queen changes him into a succession of terrifying creatures.

■ **The Indian prince Siddhartha Gautama** (563–483 BC) left behind all his riches, and wandered the world until he found the secret of true happiness. He became known as the Buddha.

■ **King Conchobar of Ulster locked** the Celtic heroine Deirdre in a castle. She managed to escape with her lover, the king's nephew, but they were both eventually murdered. Two yew trees grew out of their graves, and their branches entwined in an embrace forever.

Tam Lin

A Scottish folktale

Carterhaugh Wood was thick, green and dark, and people said it was the home of fairy folk. One bright summer's day, Janet, the earl's daughter, made up her mind to go and explore it for herself. She crept out of the castle and set off down a narrow path, deep into the woods. Birds sang in the trees, frogs croaked under rocks, and rabbits, mice and squirrels scurried through the bushes. No sign of little people so far, thought Janet to herself, keeping her wits about her just in case.

After a while, Janet reached a small stone well in the middle of a clearing. There were roses climbing all over it – far more beautiful than any in the castle gardens – and she bent to pick one.

No sooner had the stem broken off in her hand than Janet heard a voice. "Who said you could come here into our wood and pick one of our roses?"

Janet straightened up with a start and turned around. There before her stood the most handsome young knight she had ever seen. He was so charming that she quite forgot about fairy folk. Tossing her hair, she replied, "How dare you speak to me like that! These woods belong to my father, the earl. I'll go where I choose and pick whatever flowers I like."

Delight sparkled in the young man's eyes at her bold answer and he threw back his head and laughed. "I am Tam Lin," the knight said, taking Janet's hands and spinning her round, "and today you shall stay here in the forest with me and we shall play."

All day long, Tam Lin and Janet wandered through Carterhaugh Wood. They danced and sang, and by the evening, they were in love.

As dusk began to fall, Tam Lin reluctantly announced, "And now we must say farewell."

"I will not return to the castle without you," Janet vowed. "You must come with me and I will beg my father to let you stay."

"I cannot leave the wood," replied Tam Lin sadly. "I was once human, but many years ago, when I was riding through the forest, the Queen of the Fairies caught and enchanted me. Now I am an elf-knight, and I must ride by the side of the great Queen to protect her for ever more. I only wish that I could be a man again, for then I would surely marry you."

"Is there no way to break the spell?" Janet sighed.

"There is," Tam Lin said gently, "but it is terrifying and perilous. You must be very brave and steadfast."

"Tell me what I must do," Janet whispered.

"This very night is Halloween," Tam Lin explained, "a night when witches, goblins and all kinds of evil creatures roam. You must go alone to Mile Cross and hide there until midnight, for then I will come riding by. First you will see a troop of riders on black horses. Then there will be a troop of riders on brown horses. Next will come riders on horses as white as milk – and in the middle of them will ride the Queen of the Fairies herself. I will be among the elf-knights at her side, and I will wear only one glove so you can find me quickly among the throng. When you see me, you must run to my horse, seize its bridle and drag me down. You must then hold me fast, no matter what happens. The fairy folk will cast all sorts of spells on me to try to keep me. You will be in mortal danger, but if you have the strength and courage not to let go, the enchantment will at last be broken and I will be yours." Tam Lin took Janet's hand. "Do you think you can do all this?" he asked quietly.

"Yes," whispered Janet. "Yes, I can."

Later that night, when everyone else was safely inside the castle with the doors and windows barred, Janet wrapped her travelling cape around her and stole away into the darkness. It was bleak and black on the moor at Mile Cross. Shivering with both cold and fear, she found a hiding place and waited. Just before the stroke of midnight, she heard the thunder of hooves. Her blood ran cold. Out of the night appeared hundreds of black horses, bridles jangling and manes flying. On their backs were witches with sunken faces and dead, staring eyes.

Next, the brown horses galloped past, whinnying and snorting. The wrinkled goblins that rode them whipped them with willow switches, and clutched the reins with wizened fingers.

Then the white horses came like glowing ghosts through the gloom, wild-eyed and foaming at the mouth. At the centre of the riders, Janet saw the beautiful Queen of the Fairies, sitting tall and proud. Quickly, Janet searched for a rider with only one glove. Plucking up all her courage, she plunged in among the pounding hooves, pulled down the enchanted elf-knight and held Tam Lin to herself as tight as she could.

The Queen of the Fairies sent up an unearthly wail that tore through the darkness. Hundreds of riders stopped and thundered towards them, shrieking and howling.

Suddenly Janet felt Tam Lin grow in her arms and she realized she was holding a huge, hairy bear. Standing on its hind legs, the bear gave a deafening roar. Still she held him fast, and he became a hissing snake, coiling itself tightly aroung her. Still she clutched him in her arms, and he transformed into an angry, snapping wolf with teeth as sharp as swords. Still she held on tight, and he

turned into a blazing branch that burnt her flesh. Still Janet
refused to let go, and in a flash of cold lightning she saw she was at
last holding a man.

As she wrapped Tam Lin in her cloak, a haunting cry came
from the Queen of the Fairies. "Tam Lin, I would rather have
changed your eyes to wood and your heart to stone than lost you!"
Then suddenly the wild hunt was gone, disappearing into the
night. Janet and Tam Lin were left alone on the dark, windy moor.
Slowly, hand in hand, they made their way home to the castle, and
lived happily ever after.

Health and healing

- **The Navajo tribe of Native Americans** made coloured sand pictures of spirits, which they believed had the power to heal.

- **Iroquois Native American** myth tells how a tribe was once dying of illness. The animals prayed to the Supreme Spirit, who showed them a spring of healing waters.

- **In Hindu myth** Yama-Kumar was a famous doctor. His father, the lord of death, told him if he would be able to heal each of his patients.

- **Medieval myth says that the Mandrake plant** was thought to have healing powers. However, when it was pulled out of the ground, it gave a scream that drove people mad.

- **Legend says that the Brazilian Jose Arigo** (1918–1971) had miraculous psychic powers, enabling him to perform many operations, such as eye surgery, without any medical training or anaesthetic.

- **The Japanese god of medicine**, Sukuna-Biko, was so small that he could rest on a stalk of the grass, millet.

◀ *The Hemba people of Zaire carved wooden statues of their dead ancestors called* singiti. *They believed that by making offerings to the statues, they connected with their ancestor spirits. This would then give them power to heal illnesses.*

▶ *Mandrake root is famous for being a chief ingredient in witches' brews. According to legend, it was only safe to pull the plant out of the ground after performing a special ritual in the moonlight.*

■ **According to Greek myth**, when the sea goddess Thetis had a baby boy by a mortal, she tried to save the child from harm by dipping him in the river Styx. The sacred waters protected the baby everywhere except the one heel she was holding. The child grew up to be the hero Achilles.

■ **Asclepius, the Greek god of healing**, was taught the arts of medicine and surgery by a wise centaur called Chiron.

■ **In ancient Persian myth**, the hero Thrita could protect humans from disease and death because his prayers brought forth plants of healing.

■ **The Inuit god of healing** was Eeyeekalduk. He was depicted as a tiny old man who lived inside a pebble.

Yama-Kumar and the Healing Gift

An Indian legend

Take heed! Live a good life. Be kind and honest. Be respectful to the gods and to each other. For then, when you pass from the bright land of the living into the dark underground kingdom of the dead, you will have no fear of facing the lord of death, Yama.

When Yama examines your soul, he will smile upon you, whisper words of comfort, and send you on your way to one of the blessed, joyful heavens. But if you spend your time on this earth doing evil, spreading misery and causing people pain, then prepare to grovel before Yama and quake with terror. He will banish you to the deepest dungeons of his realm for punishment, and he will harden his heart against your screams and begging, for it will be too late for repentance or forgiveness.

Sometimes the just, fair Lord Yama wanders among the living and observes how his future subjects are paving their way to his kingdom, with either good or bad deeds. Concealing his true nature behind a human disguise, no one would suspect that he is anything other than an ordinary man.

Once, on one of Yama's journeys through the land of the living, he met a beautiful mortal woman and fell in love. The woman had no idea that she was being wooed by the ruler of the underworld. Overcome by his charms, the unsuspecting woman became the wife of the lord of death. Yama was delighted, although his happiness proved to be short-lived. His new bride soon became difficult and quarrelsome. Yama was horrified to find himself nagged all day long. His wife made his life a misery.

The couple were thrilled when a baby son came along, and they named him Yama-Kumar. However, to the proud father's dismay, his wife became even more bad-tempered and demanding. There came a day when the lord of death could stand his wife's scolding, screeching, shrieking voice no longer. He vanished, fleeing back to his underground realm. His wife was mystified – and determined to track her absconded husband down and make his life a hundred times more miserable.

Yama could not forget his little son, who he loved very much. From the safety of his underground kingdom, he kept a careful eye on the boy and watched him as he grew up. He was dismayed to see that his wife was not looking after the boy as she should. She either ignored him, or burdened him with boring, tedious chores. Yama-Kumar grew up without learning anything. By the time he was a young man, his father was very concerned that he had no way of making a living for himself. The ruler of the underworld decided he had to help his son, and one night, he appeared to Yama-Kumar in a dream.

"Do not be afraid," he whispered into Yama-Kumar's sleeping mind. "I am the lord of death, but I am also your father. I want to give you a very special gift. Work hard to become a doctor, learning all about medicinal herbs and plants, and I will bestow on you the power of healing. You will be able to cure anyone who is ill – unless you see me sitting at your patient's head, waiting to catch their soul, for this means that they will surely die."

When Yama-Kumar woke up, he was full of excitement. Sure enough, he did as his father had instructed and threw himself into studying medicine. He was so keen that he became a doctor in half the usual time. Yama-Kumar quickly discovered that the lord of death kept his promise. He seemed to be able to cure anyone, no matter how ill they were, no matter how unusual the problem was. Even if other doctors declared the patient a hopeless case, Yama-Kumar could cure them – unless, of course, he saw his father sitting grimly at the patient's head. Yama-Kumar became famous far and wide, and was soon known as the greatest doctor in all the land.

After some years, Yama-Kumar was called to the royal palace itself. The king and queen's beloved daughter had fallen ill, and now they feared she was dying. As Yama-Kumar entered the patient's bedroom, his heart sank. There was the shadowy figure of his father, sitting at her head. Yama-Kumar looked at the beautiful young princess lying in front of him and listened to the sobbing of the king and queen, and all the courtiers, who loved her very much. He bowed his head and prayed, pleading with his father not to take her. The lord of death sighed. "She can have three days more, my son," he murmured, and faded silently away.

The king and queen had, of course, seen and heard nothing. "Take heart," Yama-Kumar told them, "I cannot promise, but I am going to do my very best to heal your daughter." For two days and nights, he sat at the pale girl's bedside, wracking his brains to come up with a plan to save her. On the third day, Yama-Kumar finally saw the shape of his father looming into view before him.

"Beware, father!" he cried, before the lord of death could take the princess. "Allow this young woman to live to a ripe old age or I shall tell my mother who you really are and where she can find you."

Yama stopped and thought about the terrible threat. A cold shiver ran down his spine. "So be it, my son," he nodded, and disappeared hastily into the shadows.

Yama-Kumar immediately set about curing the princess with his herbs and medicines. By the time she was well again, they had fallen deeply in love. The king and queen were delighted to marry their daughter to the talented young doctor who had saved her life. And Yama-Kumar and the princess lived happily together forever.

Animal tales

■ **In Cherokee and Creek Native American myth**, food was once so scarce that bears offered to be hunted for meat and skins.

■ **A Scottish legend tells how a faithful dog**, Bobby, guarded his master's grave in Greyfriars churchyard, Edinburgh, from 1858 until his own death 14 years later.

■ **According to Roman myth**, the hedgehog emerged from its burrow on 2 February. If it saw its shadow in the sunlight, it would be scared and go back into its burrow. This meant that there would be six more weeks of winter. The American ritual of Groundhog Day is based on a similar belief.

■ **A story recorded by a Greek slave called Aesop** tells how a man called Androcles was thrown to a lion in an amphitheatre. However, the lion refused to eat him because Androcles had once pulled a thorn from its injured paw.

■ **In 1912, Edgar Rice Burroughs wrote a book** about a child who was brought up by gorillas in the jungle. The legend of Tarzan was born.

◄ *Legend has it that a dog called Bobby laid by his master's grave in Edinburgh until he himself died many years later.*

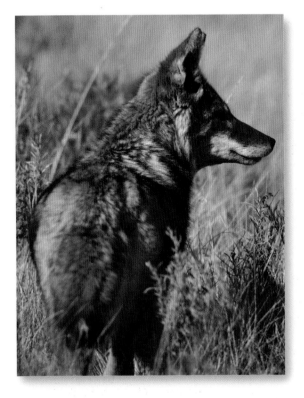

◄ *Many native American myths involve the coyote, a wily trickster. Mischievous and destructive, he delighted in causing chaos in the world.*

■ **Christian stories say that Saint Francis of Assisi** communicated with animals, birds and fish, and preached to them just as he did to humans.

■ **The legendary hero** the Lone Ranger rode a faithful white horse that he famously summoned with the shout, "Hi-yo, Silver!"

■ **In Russian myth**, a wise grey wolf helps a Tsar's son called Ivan to search for the legendary firebird.

■ **An Inuit myth says** that the Supreme Spirit made the bowhead whale their best friend. He allowed the Inuits to hunt the creature for food, skins and tools to survive.

■ **Traditional stories told by the Maya people** describe the adventures of a pair of hero twins, Xbalanque and Hunahpu, who turned their brother into a monkey because he was stealing their food.

The Firebird

A Russian folk tale

L ong ago in Russia, in the days when witches lurked in the forests, dragons flew over the plains, and demons hid in the mountains, there lived a lord called Tsar Andronovich who owned a magnificent garden. At the centre of the garden lay a beautiful orchard, and in the middle of the orchard grew Tsar Andronovich's favourite tree – a tree that grew golden apples. No one was allowed to touch the golden apple tree except for Tsar Andronovich himself. But one night, an amazing firebird with wings of flame and eyes of crystal came blazing into the orchard and stole some of the precious fruit.

"A fortune to whoever brings me this amazing firebird alive." Tsar Andronovich declared the very next day. "This creature is even more splendid than the golden apples she has been stealing!"

Half an hour later, the Tsar's three sons galloped out of the gates in search of the firebird. The eldest and middle son, Dimitri and Vassili, thundered off together. They had agreed to split the fortune between them. The youngest son, Ivan, went off sadly on his own.

Ivan rode for three days and nights without seeing any sign of the firebird. His food and water began to run low, and his horse was exhausted. Just as Ivan was thinking things couldn't get much worse, he heard a blood-curdling howl and out of a dark forest ran a huge grey wolf. Ivan's horse shot away from under him, throwing him into the dirt. But it didn't escape very far. The grey wolf sprang onto it and gobbled it up.

"Eat me quickly and have done!" Ivan cried at the panting beast.

"I am not going to eat you," grinned the wolf. "I have to repay you for eating your very tasty horse! Now, you look worn out. Ride on me and I will take you where you want to go."

Ivan was too tired and lonely to argue. He climbed onto the grey wolf's back and explained all about his quest to find the firebird. He had hardly finished speaking when the grey wolf leapt away like an arrow. It seemed only a few seconds before they halted at a stone wall.

"Ivan, climb this wall and you will see the firebird in a golden cage," the wolf explained. "Take the firebird, but whatever you do, do not steal the golden cage."

Trembling, Ivan clambered over the wall and found himself in a courtyard below. Hanging from a tree was a golden cage with the firebird inside, just as the wolf had said. Ivan crept over to it, opened the jewelled door, and drew out the beautiful firebird. 'I really need the cage as well,' thought Ivan. He reached up and unhooked the cage. At that moment, ear-splitting alarm bells rang and guards rushed in from all sides. They dragged Ivan to their master, Tsar Dolmat.

"You must pay dearly for trying to steal my precious firebird," boomed Tsar Dolmat, his face dark with anger. Then he rubbed his beard and thought for a second. "UNLESS," he added, "you go to the ends of the earth and bring me the horse with the golden mane. If you do this, I will give you the firebird with pleasure."

Ivan crept back to the grey wolf in shame. But his friend simply said, "Ride on me and I will take you where you want to go."

The grey wolf sprang away faster than the wind. It seemed only a couple of minutes before they stopped outside some stables.

"Ivan, go into these stables and take the horse with the golden mane," the wolf told him. "But whatever you do, do not steal its golden bridle."

Cautiously, Ivan edged into the stables, crept up to the horse with the golden mane, and began to lead it out of its stall. 'I really need the bridle as well,' thought Ivan. He lifted down the bridle and a clanging peal of bells broke the silence. Soldiers dashed into the stable and hauled Ivan away to see their master, Tsar Afron.

"You must pay dearly for trying to steal my wonderful horse with the golden mane," raged Tsar Afron, shaking with fury. "UNLESS," he added, "you go to the other side of the world and bring me Tasha the Beautiful to be my bride. If you do this, I will gladly give you the horse with the golden mane."

When Ivan returned empty-handed, the wolf did not scold. He simply said, "Ride on me and I will take you where you want to go."

Ivan jumped onto the grey wolf and he sped away to the other side of the world as quick as lightning. It seemed only an hour before they drew up outside a glorious palace.

"Ivan, this time I am going to be the one who goes inside and you are going to be the one who waits," said the wolf and he sprang over the palace wall with one mighty bound. Ivan hardly had time to draw breath before the wolf came springing over again – this time with Tasha the Beautiful tossed onto his back. Ivan leapt onto the wolf and they were off through the air like a shooting star.

By the time the three arrived back at Tsar Afron's home, the grey wolf was highly surprised to find Ivan weeping bitterly.

"Why are you crying?" the grey wolf asked.

"I have fallen in love with Tasha," Ivan protested, "and she has fallen in love with me. I cannot let her go."

The grey wolf looked at Tasha the Beautiful and she nodded sadly.

"Oh very well," sighed the grey wolf. "I will turn myself into the form of Tasha the Beautiful. You can present me to Tsar Afron in her place and he will give you the horse with the golden mane. When you are two mountains away, think of me and I will be back at your side."

And so, Tsar Afron was tricked and soon Ivan was once again mounted on the grey wolf while his sweetheart, Tasha the Beautiful, rode on the horse with the golden mane.

As they drew near the villa of Tsar Dolmat, Ivan sighed a deep sigh. "Oh grey wolf," he began, "I would so like to keep this horse with the golden mane. Would you turn into the form of the horse, as you disguised yourself as Tasha before? Then I could take you to Tsar Dolmat and win the firebird. When I am two forests away, I will think of you and you will return back to my side."

The grey wolf looked at Ivan and bowed slightly. "For you, I will do this." And so it came to pass and Tsar Dolmat was tricked. Ivan once again mounted the grey wolf while his sweetheart, Tasha the Beautiful, rode on the horse with the golden mane and carried the firebird.

By and by, the companions came to the very spot where the grey wolf had set upon Ivan's horse and eaten it. Then it was the grey wolf's turn to sigh a deep sigh. "Well, Ivan, here I took a horse from you and here I now return you with another horse, a beautiful bride and a firebird, too! You no longer need me and I must go." And with that, the grey wolf disappeared into the woods.

Ivan and Tasha went on their way in sadness, weeping for their lost friend. As they stopped to rest, the two figures of Dimitri and Vassily crept out of the shadows. They had returned from their travels empty-handed and were enraged to find their little brother not only with the firebird, but also with Tasha the Beautiful. In their bitterness, the brothers drew their swords and stabbed Ivan where he lay, dreaming. Then they swept up Tasha the Beautiful and the firebird, and were off to their father's mansion to pretend that the treasures were theirs. "Breathe a word of this and we'll kill you, too," they hissed into Tasha's ear, making her shake with sorrow and fear.

Ivan's body lay lifeless and cold. Snow began to cover him like a thick blanket. Birds and woodland creatures slowly crept closer to find out what was lying so silent and still in the freezing weather – and among them came a grey wolf with yellow eyes and drooling jaws. He stalked right up to Ivan's body and sniffed all around.

Throwing his head back, he gave a spine-chilling howl. Slowly and gently, the wolf began to lick the wound in Ivan's chest. And suddenly, Ivan sat up and began to shiver.

"Why am I asleep in this snowstorm?" he asked the grey wolf.

"Ride on me," came the gruff voice, "and I will take you where you want to go."

"Home," whispered Ivan into his friend's ear, "I want to go home." And no sooner had he finished saying the words than they were there.

Of course, when Tsar Andronovich learnt the truth, he threw the wicked Dimitri and Vassily in a dungeon. Ivan and Tasha the Beautiful were married – Ivan rode his faithful grey wolf to the wedding and Tasha arrived on the horse with the golden mane. As for Tsar Andronovich, well, he got his precious firebird after all – and he loved her so much, he even let her eat the golden apples from his favourite tree whenever she wanted.

Eternal life

■ **The ancient Chinese religion**, Taoism, teaches belief in eight immortals who discovered a magical elixir of life, allowing them to live forever.

■ **In Medieval Europe**, early scientists called alchemists strove to create an elixir of life that would cure all illnesses.

■ **The Celtic god Govannon is a blacksmith** who also brews a mead of eternal life.

■ **The mischievous Chinese spirit**, Monkey, was once appointed Guardian of the Garden of Immortal Peaches – but he ate all the heavenly fruit and became immortal himself.

■ **In Arabic**, *khuld* means eternal life. Islamic stories teach that all souls are immortal – some will go to heaven and others will go to hell.

■ **In Roman mythology**, Jupiter punished a traitor called Janus by giving him immortality but taking away his freedom to move. Janus was made to stand forever as heaven's gatekeeper.

■ **Sengen is the Japanese goddess of blossom** and the sacred mountain Fujiyama. She guards the secret Well of Eternal Youth.

◄ *Egyptian gods are sometimes pictured holding a symbol called an ankh as though it were a key. This symbolized the opening of the gates of death to immortality.*

◄ The ancient Egyptians wore pendants showing Maat, the goddess of law and order. They believed that after death there is a test – your heart is weighed against Maat. If you passed this test, your immortal soul would enter paradise. If you failed the test, your heart would be devoured by the beast Ammut, and you would not survive the afterlife.

■ **In Chinese myth**, the birds, cranes, are used as symbols of immortality.

■ **In Greek myth**, ambrosia was the food of the gods. Anyone who ate it became immortal.

■ **The ancient Greek god Heracles** was thought to be superhuman. He performed many dangerous tasks, such as capturing the beast Cerberus. As a reward, he was made immortal.

▶ According to legend, the centaur Chiron had the gift of eternal life, but after being hit by a poisoned arrow, he gave up his immortality for the life of another and became the constellation Centaurus.

Struggle with fate

■ **According to Gypsy belief**, there are three female spirits of fate. Two are good, but one seeks to harm humans.

■ **Norse myth tells of three women** who decide the fate of humans – the Norns.

■ **The Greeks and Romans** also believed in three women who set destiny, called the Fates.

■ **The Vikings thought that** even their warrior gods were fated to die one day.

■ **Although the classical gods** and goddesses often helped their favourite mortals, they never tried to change their destined deaths.

■ **Greek mythology says** that the god Apollo used an oracle at Delphi in Greece to tell the people what was fated to happen.

■ **Today in Italy**, you can still see the cave at Cumae where a famous seer called the Sibyl spoke of things fated to happen.

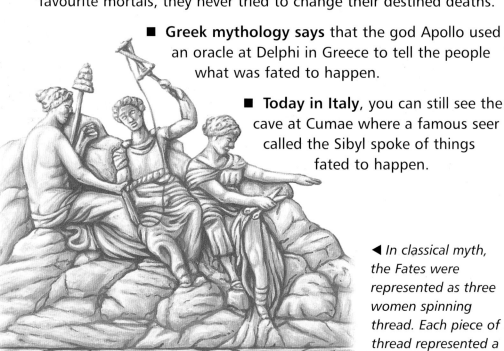

◀ *In classical myth, the Fates were represented as three women spinning thread. Each piece of thread represented a human life. The Fates decided how long or short it should be.*

▲ *Historians think that Delphi was a sacred site in Greece long before the worship of the god Apollo in ancient times. Female figurines dating back to the 12th century BC have been found, indicating that an early earth goddess was worshipped there.*

■ **The Fon god of fate, Legba**, is shown as an old man leaning on a stick, which he uses to prop up the universe.

■ **Slavic peoples believed** that the spirits of female ancestors appeared at the cradle of a newborn baby to decide its destiny.

■ **The Celts did not fear fate**, as they believed that death was merely a passage from this life to a happy land where everyone lived in eternal bliss.

Warnings and curses

■ **Celtic peoples believed** that if anyone heard the wail of a spirit woman called a Banshee, they would soon die.

■ **In Greek myth**, the inventor Daedalus made wings for himself and his son Icarus to escape from prison. Daedalus warned Icarus not to fly too near to the sun, but Icarus forgot. His wings burned and he plunged to his death in the ocean.

■ **According to the Eastern Orthodox Church**, the body of anyone bound by a curse will not decay, so they cannot find peace.

■ **In 1798, Coleridge wrote a poem** called *The Rime of the Ancient Mariner* based on an ancient curse – any sailor who shoots a huge seabird called an albatross brings doom upon his crew.

■ **Medieval legends say** that the Wandering Jew was a man who mocked Jesus when he was carrying his cross. Jesus cursed him to walk the earth until the end of time.

■ **Deirdre was the beautiful, tragic heroine** of many Irish legends. She was doomed from birth to bring death and misery. To prevent this, the king of Ireland kept her prisoner, but Deirdre escaped with the man she loved.

▶ *The word banshee comes from the Irish Gaelic,* bean sidhe, *which literally means 'woman of the fairy mound'.*

▲ The Rime of the Ancient Mariner *warned that any sailor who shot an albatross brought doom upon his crew.*

■ **The Greek god Zeus cursed** the prophet Phineas for being too truthful to mortals. Whenever Phineas sat down to eat, creatures called Harpies swooped down and snatched his food away.

■ **In 387 BC, a Roman called Caedicius** heard a voice for several days warning that the city walls should be strengthened. The Roman authorities did not believe him. Not long afterwards, invading armies of Gauls arrived and found the city almost undefended.

■ **According to German myth**, if you see your own double, or *doppelganger*, it is a warning that you will soon die.

■ **Christians believe** that the Curse of Eve is the pain women suffer during childbirth.

Daedalus and Icarus

A Greek myth

Daedalus was renowned all over Greece for being a famous craftsman and architect. People from far and wide travelled to Daedalus' workshop in Athens to beg for his help in designing stunning landmarks and amazing inventions. No one could come up with such brilliant new ideas as Daedalus … until one of his apprentices, his nephew Talos, started to amaze everyone with his own talents. Daedalus should have been proud of his young protégé, but he wasn't. He was unbearably jealous. In cold blood, Daedalus lured his rival to the roof of the great temple, then pushed him over the edge to his death.

The Athenian court banished the great inventor from the city forever. Daedalus fled to the island of Crete, which was ruled by the mighty King Minos. Daedalus knew that Minos would be delighted to have the world's most famous inventor at his court, and would pay him handsomely for his expertise.

One of the first tasks King Minos set Daedalus was to devise a lair for a monstrous creature called the Minotaur, which was half-man, half-bull. Daedalus created an underground labyrinth of criss-crossing corridors and alleys that twisted and turned their way to dead-ends. The Minotaur was let loose to roam about in its depths.

Every year, King Minos fed the monster by forcing a group of young Athenian men and women into the labyrinth and leaving them to be hunted down and devoured.

From then on Daedalus' life became better and better. He fell in love with a royal lady-in-waiting and was thrilled when one year later, she bore him a son who they named Icarus. At last, Daedalus was happy and content.

One fateful day an Athenian hero, Theseus, managed to kill the Minotaur and emerge alive from the maze. King Minos was outraged, and Daedalus and Icarus hid themselves away, afraid of his wrath. Daedalus decided that they had to escape from the island – but it was not going to be easy. Minos' soldiers stood guard at all the sea ports, harbours and coves, and would catch them wherever they tried to board a boat. Daedalus wracked his brains to come up with an escape plan. In the end, he could only think of one way – they would have to flee by air.

Daedalus set about fashioning huge wings for himself and his son. He collected sackfuls of feathers, and glued them into shape with wax. It was a long, painstaking job, but finally Daedalus gave the wings a careful inspection and pronounced them ready. He strapped one pair onto his son and the other onto himself. Then the intrepid pair prepared to jump off a high cliff.

"Listen carefully, my son," ordered Daedalus. "Do not soar too high, or the sun will scorch your wings. And do not dip too low, or the spray of the sea will soak them. Just follow me and do as I do."

Daedalus shut his eyes and prayed a silent prayer to the gods. Then he and Icarus launched themselves off the cliff. It worked! Wings outstretched, they were lifted aloft on the breeze, gliding over the ocean, floating away from Crete and cruel King Minos.

Icarus whooped, wide-eyed with excitement. He felt such a thrill that he totally forgot his father's warning. He soared upwards and hovered in the heat of the sun. Then his joy turned to pain as burning wax began to drip down his arms. "Help me, father!" he screamed, as he realized what was happening. "My wings are melting!"

Daedalus was horrified, but there was nothing he could do. He watched, helpless, as his son dropped out of the sky and splashed into the sea, struggling, spluttering and sinking.

The gods had chosen to punish the great inventor for murdering his young nephew. And even though the master craftsman made it to safety, he lived for the rest of his days with a broken heart that not even he could mend.

Burial beliefs

- **The Greek god of the underworld**, Hades, taught burial practices to mortals, to show respect for the dead.

- **The Bushpeople of Botswana believe** that Gauna, or death, taught them burial rituals in order to keep ghosts in their graves.

- **Zoroastrians believe that dead bodies** provide a home for Angra Mainy, the force of evil. The bodies are left out for vultures because the earth is too sacred for burial.

- **In Java, stories claim** that anyone who wishes to receive a message from a spirit should spend the night alone in the mortuary.

- **Arthurian legend says** that Lancelot once captured a castle called Dolorous Gard. When he explored it, he found a tomb with his own name on it. It was where he was destined to be buried.

▼ *Tribal peoples in Indonesia try to impress the gods, so their spirit is allowed into heaven. After a party that goes on for days, the corpse is laid in a burial cave, to become part of a display of hundreds of skulls and skeletons.*

▶ *In Mexico, 1 November is celebrated as the Day of the Dead, when people believe their dead loved ones will visit them. Shops sell skeleton toys, cake coffins and bread bones, which people buy to leave as offerings for the spirits.*

■ **In Finnish myth**, the goddess of death and decay, Kalma, is believed to haunt graves, snatching the flesh of the dead.

■ **The Greeks and Romans covered a dead body**, or its ashes, with earth – even a symbolic couple of handfuls was enough. If left uncovered, the dead person's soul would not find its way into the underworld.

■ **When the Greek hero, Jason,** was fleeing from the king of Colchis, the witch Medea cut up the king's son (her brother) and scattered pieces of his body behind Jason's ship. The king stopped to collect the pieces in order to give his son a proper burial, so Jason and the Argonauts escaped.

■ **Hindu stories say** that if the ashes of a dead person are scattered on the river Ganges at the holy city of Varanasi, their soul will be nearer to breaking the endless cycle of death and rebirth, and thus closer to heaven.

■ **At a Chinese funeral**, mourners burn fake money. This is as an offering to the gods of the underworld, so that they will allow the dead person to pass through and reach heaven.

Legendary 'baddies'

- **The Roman Emperor Caligula** was an evil tyrant who hated his own people and delighted in torturing them. He was born in AD 12 and murdered in AD 41.

- **Ghengis Khan was a ruthless military leader** who united the Mongol tribes into an empire around AD 1200. He destroyed anyone or anything that stood in his way.

- **The most famous American gangster**, Al Capone, was born in Brooklyn, New York in 1899. He lived a life of crime in Chicago and died in 1947 – not through mob warfare, but from ill health.

- **Edward Teach is better known as the pirate**, Blackbeard. His career on the high seas only lasted two years before he was killed in 1718. During that time he attacked so many ships that he became the most famous pirate ever.

- **Anne Bonny and Mary Read were two women pirates** caught on the ship, *Revenge*, in 1720. They were sentenced to be hanged, but Anne disappeared from prison, and Mary died of fever.

- **Attila was a savage warrior** who united the Hun tribes of Eastern Europe into a mighty empire in the 5th century. The Romans called him 'the Scourge of God' because of the destruction he wreaked.

- **In Victorian times, a penniless barber** called Sweeney Todd lived in Fleet Street in London. He killed his customers and stole their money, and a woman neighbour made the bodies into pies.

- **Ghede (or Baron Samedi) is the sinister god** of the dead in Haitian Voodoo mythology. He wears dark glasses, a black tailcoat and top hat.

- **European myth tells of a man called Faustus** who sold his soul to the devil in return for earthly power and riches.

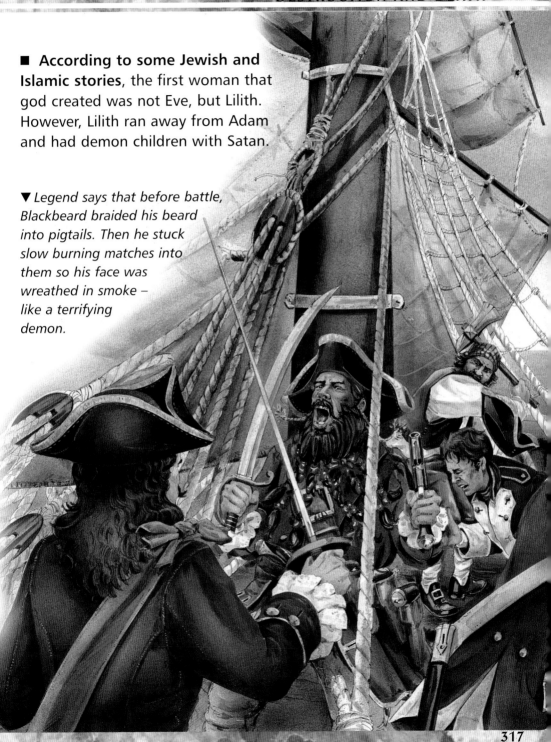

■ **According to some Jewish and Islamic stories**, the first woman that god created was not Eve, but Lilith. However, Lilith ran away from Adam and had demon children with Satan.

▼ *Legend says that before battle, Blackbeard braided his beard into pigtails. Then he stuck slow burning matches into them so his face was wreathed in smoke – like a terrifying demon.*

Wrath and punishment

- **Egyptian myth says that illnesses** were brought into the world by the lion-headed goddess, Sekhmet, to punish humans who were turning against the sun god, Ra.

- **Once, a Greek nymph called Echo** annoyed Zeus to such an extent due to her constant talking, that he took away her speech. From then on, she could only repeat the words of others.

- **German legend tells of a mysterious musician** called the Pied Piper who rid the town of Hamelin of a plague of rats in 1284. When the townspeople refused to pay him, the Pied Piper lured their children away as punishment.

- **In Greek myth**, an evil king called Tantalus was punished in the underworld by being chained up near to water and food. Every time he reached for it, it moved away.

- **Hittite myth says** that when the bad-tempered fertility god Telepinu is angry, the world is punished and nothing will grow.

▶ *This Viking carving shows the Norse trickster Loki. Half-god, half-giant, he was often friendly, fun company for the gods, but ultimately turned malicious.*

▶ *People from different cultures believe that ghosts bring messages from beyond the grave. Some myths suggest that ghosts predict future dangers. Others say that ghosts warn sinners to change their ways, or face a terrible punishment after death.*

■ **Sisyphus, a king of Corinth, was condemned** to the underworld when he exposed Zeus as a adulterer. He had to spend an eternity continuously rolling a boulder up a hill.

■ **The Greeks believed** in a goddess responsible for punishing wrongdoers, called Nemesis.

■ **In Chinese myth**, Buddha punished the naughty Monkey by making him accompany a young priest on a journey from India to bring Buddhist teachings to China.

■ **The wicked Norse god Loki** was punished by being bound to a rock in chains made from his own son's body. A snake was then fixed to drip venom on his head for the rest of time.

■ **According to Greek myth**, Zeus punished the Titan Prometheus for giving humans the secret of fire. Zeus nailed him to a mountain and ordered an eagle to tear out his liver. This happened each day for eternity.

The Pied Piper of Hamelin

A German legend

*I*magine what it would be like to live in a town overrun by rats. Rats in the streets, shops and gardens. Rats in the town hall, hospital and police station. Rats in the cafés, restaurants and library. Rats in your school corridors, classroom and desk. Rats in your kitchen, bath and even your bed! Well, that's what it was like to live in the town of Hamelin on the river Weser.

No one knew where the rats had come from or how they had managed to take over the town in such numbers. The townspeople of Hamelin were desperate to be rid of them. They couldn't eat without rats nibbling off their plates. They couldn't get dressed without uncovering rats nestling in their clothes and boots. They couldn't put their babies down to sleep without finding rats cuddled up in the cradles. They couldn't sit down without shaking out rats from the chair cushions. They couldn't go shopping without rats scurrying over their shoes. They couldn't even chat to each other in comfort, for the noise of all the squeaking and scampering! So you can see why the mayor put up a poster outside the town hall saying:

There will be a reward of
ONE THOUSAND GUILDERS
to anyone who can get rid of the rats.

Yes, one thousand guilders! More than triple what the mayor himself earned in a lifetime. Everyone began to imagine what they would do with such a huge fortune – but of course, they could only dream. No one had the first idea how to begin claiming their town back from the rats.

By the time the stranger came knocking on the door of the town hall, the mayor was panic-stricken. He would have listened to anybody who said they could help. So when the stranger announced confidently, "I can get rid of all the rats for you," the mayor didn't worry too much about the stranger's odd, multicoloured costume. The mayor paid no attention to the stranger's extraordinarily long fingers and the unusual pipe that hung on a cord round his neck. The mayor didn't think too much about the sad smile on the stranger's face or the wistful gleam in his eyes. They mayor simply beamed with relief. "GREAT! When can you begin?"

"Right now," replied the stranger, and he raised his pipe to his lips. Off he went, out of the town hall and into the street, playing a lilting tune that filled the air. Instantly, all over town, the rats stopped scuffling, pricked up their ears, and listened. For the first time in many, many months, the rats were silent. Then the scampering and squeaking began again, as the rats followed the hypnotic tune.

The townspeople couldn't believe their eyes. All through the town strolled the strange man, his fingers continually moving on his pipe and the haunting notes rippling through the air. Out of the houses swarmed the rats. Out of every garden and gutter, out of every nook and cranny, they came streaming. From doorways and windows, down stairwells and through streets, out of passages and alleyways, over rooftops and along roads, the rats came hurrying after the extraordinary musician. And he didn't stop playing all the way to the river, where he dipped one brightly coloured foot into the rushing waters. Suddenly, thousands of rats began to plunge off the bank into the river. He didn't stop playing as the rats struggled and sank in the swirling waters. He didn't stop playing until the very last rat had drowned.

The church bells rang out in celebration and all over the town mighty cheering rose up. The people started hugging each other, the children began dancing and singing – and the musical saviour strode quietly back to the town hall to collect his reward.

"My one thousand guilders, if you please," he asked the mayor calmly.

The mayor just smiled what he thought was a charming smile. Now the rats were dead and gone, he certainly didn't plan on giving away what was nearly the entire contents of the town council bank account.

"Come, come now, my dear fellow," the mayor coaxed. "One thousand guilders is somewhat over-the-top for playing a pretty ditty on a tin whistle, surely you'll agree! Why don't we settle on fifty guilders? I'll even throw in a nice bronze medal and put up a statue of you and me together in the market place."

Without saying a word, the stranger simply turned on his heel and walked out into the street. As he went, he once more lifted the pipe to his lips. But this time, he played a different tune. Enchanting notes rippled all around, stirring the air. From all over the town, the children came dancing down the roads, running and leaping towards the magical sound.

The men and women of Hamelin were struck still with horror as the children swept past them and were gone through the streets. Following the strange melody, the children were led along the banks of the river Weser. They skipped happily along a narrow, forgotten path that led up to a steep, craggy mountain.

With a burst of airy notes, a little door appeared in the mountain slope and the children went inside. The stunned townspeople could hear the echo of the pipe and the children's laughter grow fainter and fainter as they went deeper and deeper into the earth. Then suddenly, the little door slammed shut and disappeared. The children were gone – all except for one little boy who was lame, and so hadn't been able to keep up with the others. He stood on the mountainside and sobbed, calling out for his friends. But the little door had vanished.

No one ever saw the mysterious stranger again, known today as the Pied Piper. On sunny days, some townsfolk swore that they could hear ripples of childish laughter floating down from the mountain. And from that day to this, there has never been a single rat in the town of Hamelin.

Underworlds

▶ *Greek myth tells how Heracles'
final task was to capture the
three-headed hound Cerberus,
guarding the entrance of the
underworld. The hero dragged
him to the court of King
Eurystheus, and then returned
him to the underworld.*

■ **In every culture**, there
are myths explaining the
afterlife. Evil people are
punished by spending eternity in the underworld, which is often full
of torturous demons and devils.

■ **Ancient Greeks believed** that if a god or goddess swore an oath
on an underworld river called the Styx, they were not allowed to
break it.

■ **Another river in the underworld** was called the Lethe. Greek
myth says that spirits drank from it to forget their past lives.

■ **According to the Ainu of Japan**, all souls go to an underworld
called Pokna-Moshiri where the good are rewarded and the bad are
punished.

■ **In Welsh mythology**, the goddess Cerridwena brews a mead of
divine knowledge and inspiration in the cauldron of the
underworld.

■ **Classical myth says** that a terrifying three-headed dog called
Cerberus guarded the entrance to the underworld.

■ **Mictlan is the ninth and lowest level** of the Mayan underworld. It is the cold, dark realm of the wicked.

■ **In the mythology of Finland**, the underworld is called Tuonela. It is a place of disease and corpse-eating monsters.

■ **The queen of the Norse underworld** was Hela, the goddess of death. She was half-living, half-corpse. She ruled over the spirits of those who did not die in battle.

■ **In Libyan mythology**, the underworld is ruled by the goddess of death and prophecy, Echidne. She is half-woman, half-serpent.

▼ *According to Egyptian myth, in the ritual of the Opening of the Mouth, the jaw of the coffin was 'opened' using an adze (a tool with a bronze blade). It was believed that this would enable the deceased to speak in the afterlife. The wall painting below, from Tutankhamun's burial chamber, shows Ay performing the ceremony for the deceased king.*

Disappearances

■ **For thousands of years**, strange disappearances have occured around the world and many legends have developed to explain them. These often involve common mythical themes such as witchcraft.

■ **The legend of Lord Lucan** tells how he vanished, never to be seen again, on 7 November 1974 – the same day that his children's nanny was found murdered at their home in London, England.

■ **The beautiful Egyptian** queen, Nefertiti, was the wife of a rebel pharaoh, Akhenaten, who tried to change traditional religious beliefs and made many enemies. No one knows how she died, and her mummy has never been found.

◄ *The* Mary Celeste *was a small trading vessel bound from New York for Genoa. Her crew mysteriously disappeared without any sign of violence or emergency.*

- **In 1912, the explorer Laurence Oates** became very ill on an Antarctic expedition led by Captain Scott. He committed suicide rather than endanger his colleagues by slowing them down. Legend says that he walked out of his tent into the snow, saying, 'I am going out now. I may be some time.'

- **The explorer Roald Amundsen** was the first to reach the South Pole. In 1928 his plane crashed over the Arctic Ocean. His body was never found.

- **The Bermuda Triangle** is a large triangular area in the Atlantic Ocean, off the coast of Florida. Unexplainable phenomena have occured here – navigational systems are affected and many ships and oceans have even disappeared.

- **The legend of the *Mary Celeste*** tells of a ship found drifting in the Atlantic Ocean in December 1872. The last entry in the ship's log was 25 November. The entire crew had vanished without trace.

- **On 8 February 1983**, a legendary racehorse called Shergar was kidnapped and held to a ransom of £1.5 million pounds. However, the horse was never found and no one knows what happened to him.

- **Since the 18th century**, the legend of the Blair witch has been blamed for the mysterious disappearance of countless people in Maryland, US. The 1999 film *The Blair Witch Project* was based on these events.

- **The American pilot Amelia Earhart** went missing on 2 July 1937 on her round-the-world flight.

Vampire mythology

■ **Blood-drinking monsters** have featured in myths for thousands of years. Ancient Greeks believed in creatures called lamiae that ate children and drank blood. Stories from India from 3500 years ago tell of vampire-like creatures called Rakshasas.

■ **Modern ideas about vampires** come from Eastern Europe. They are pale-skinned 'undead' who sleep in their coffins during the day and come out at night to drink blood and turn other people into vampires.

■ **Legend has it** that by drinking blood, supernatural powers are gained.

▼ *Legend says that vampires can only attack people at night. During the day, they have to remain in the darkness of their coffins as sunlight can kill them.*

◄ *According to Christian stories, evil spirits will shrink away from the image of the dying Christ on a crucifix.*

■ **The most famous vampire** is Bram Stoker's Dracula who lived in a castle in Transylvania, Romania. The myth may have come from the Romanian tyrant, Vlad the Impaler, who was also known by the name Dracula.

■ **The 1922 German film** *Nosferatu, eine Symphonie des Grauens* (A Symphony of Horrors) is one of the most successful screen adaptations of Bram Stoker's *Dracula*. The word nosferatu is believed to be Slavonic, meaning vampire.

■ **Myths say you can ward** off vampires with crucifixes, holy water and garlic.

■ **People believe that there are three ways** to kill a vampire – drive a wooden stake through the vampire's heart, expose the vampire to sunlight, or set the vampire on fire.

■ **Around 1560**, a Slovak noblewoman called Elizabeth Bathory killed over 600 girls and drank their blood. She believed this would keep her youthful.

■ **The rare medical condition** porphyria could account for some vampire myths. It causes sensitivity to sunlight and certain foods, and makes gums deteriorate, giving the incisor teeth the appearance of 'fangs'.

■ **Vampire myths have inspired books** including Bram Stoker's *Dracula*, Ann Rice's *Interview with a Vampire*, and Stephen King's *Salem's Lot*.

Evil and death

■ **Many African tribes believe** that death entered the world by mistake. For instance, Burundi myth says that the creator was chasing death out of the world when a woman got in his way, so death escaped.

■ **In Banyarwanda myth**, the creator once hunted death. He told everyone to stay indoors, so death could not hide. But an old woman went out to hoe her vegetable garden, and death hid under her skirt and was taken inside.

■ **According to Greek myth**, a girl called Pandora was forbidden by the god Mercury to open a sealed box. She disobeyed him and released evil and sorrow into the world.

■ **Native American myths** tell that the god Coyote decided that humans should die. He regretted this bitterly when he could not save his own son from a snake bite.

■ **A Caraja myth from South America** says that the first humans lived underground and were immortal. When they discovered the beautiful land above the earth, many people stayed and lived there, even though they would one day become old and die.

◄ *The voodoo god of death, Ghede, is also known as King Cholera. In Victorian England, this symbol of death became well known as thousands died of the disease cholera.*

◄ *In the mythologies of many European countries, death is pictured as being a silent figure in a dark cloak. His hood hides his face – a skull. He sometimes carries a scythe with which he cuts short human lives, and is then called 'the Grim Reaper'.*

■ **In Norse mythology**, a giantess witch called Gullveig once entered the world of humans, bringing sin and misery.

■ **The Navajo Native Americans believed** that all evils entered the world from the east, including sickness and war.

■ **A myth from New Zealand says** that the Dawn Maiden once unknowingly committed a crime and fled to the underworld. Ever since, she has dragged people down to the land of the dead to be with her.

■ **A Sudanese myth tells** how the mother of a dead child once begged the god Ajok to bring her baby back to life. When the father found out he was horrified, and killed the child again. From then on, people could never be brought back to life.

■ **In Papua New Guinean myth**, Honoyeta was a demon that could take on the form of a human or snake. One day, one of his wives burnt his snakeskin, so he was stuck in his human form forever. As retaliation, Honoyeta brought death to humans.

Pandora's Box

A Greek myth

When the world was first created, it was a happy place with no sadness or pain. The sun shone every day and the gods came down from heaven to walk and talk with the humans who lived on earth.

One afternoon, Epimetheus and his wife, Pandora, were outside tending their flower garden when they saw the god Mercury approaching carrying a dark wooden chest. He looked hot and tired.

"My friends, would you do me a favour?" sighed Mercury. "It is so hot today and this chest is so heavy. May I leave it here for a while?"

"Of course you can," smiled Epimetheus.

Epimetheus and Mercury heaved the chest indoors. It was carved with strange markings and tied shut with golden cords.

"No one must see it," instructed Mercury anxiously. "And NO ONE under ANY circumstances must open the box."

"Don't worry," laughed
Epimetheus and Pandora,
and they waved the
god off through
the trees.

Pandora
stopped still and
frowned. "Listen, Epimetheus!"
she hissed. "Someone is whispering our names!"

Epimetheus and Pandora listened hard. At first, they heard
nothing. Then they heard the distant sound of "Epimetheus!
Pandora!" being called from outside.

"It's our friends," said Epimetheus, happily.

"Those aren't the voices I heard," she said, puzzled.

"They must have been," Epimetheus laughed. "Come on now,
let's go and see everyone."

"You go," Pandora insisted, with a frown. "I'd rather stay here
for a while."

Epimetheus shrugged, kissed Pandora on the nose, and strode
outside. As soon as he was gone, Pandora hurried over to the
strange box and waited. After only a few seconds, she heard the
whispery voices again. Maybe Pandora was imagining it. She bent
closer and put her ear to the lid. No, this time she was sure. The
box was calling to her. "Pandora!" the voices pleaded. "Let us out,

Pandora. We are trapped in here in the darkness. Please set us free."

Pandora jumped back with a start. Mercury had expressly forbade them or anyone else to open the box. Yet the voices sounded so sad.

"Pandora!" they came again. "Help us, we beg you!"

Pandora could stand it no longer. Hurriedly, she knelt down and worked at the tight golden knots. All the time, the pleading whispers filled her ears, begging for her help. At last the gleaming cords fell away. She hesitated, then took a deep breath and opened the lid.

At once, Pandora realized that she had done a terrible thing. The box had been crammed with all the evils in the world – thousands of tiny, brown, mothlike creatures that caused hurt and misery wherever they went. Now, thanks to Pandora, the evils were free! They flew up out of the chest in a great swarm and fluttered all over Pandora's skin, stinging her over and over again. For the very first time, Pandora felt pain and regret. She began to wail with despair, and all too late, she slammed the lid back down onto the box.

Outside, Epimetheus heard his wife's cries and came running. The little creatures fluttered to sting and bite him, before speeding off through the window into the world. For the first time ever, Epimetheus began to shout at his wife in anger. Pandora yelled back, and the couple realized in horror that they were arguing.

"Let me out!" interrupted a high voice. Pandora and Epimetheus grabbed onto each other in a panic. The voice was coming from inside the box. "Don't be afraid of me. Let me out and I can help you," came the voice once more.

"What do you think?" Pandora whispered to Epimetheus.

"Surely you can't do any more mischief than you already have done," he grumbled. So Pandora shut her eyes and opened Mercury's chest for a second time.

Out of the box fluttered a single shining white spirit like a butterfly. It was Hope. Pandora and Epimetheus sobbed with relief as she fluttered against their skin and soothed their stinging wounds. Then she was gone, darting out of the window and into the world after the evils.

Fortunately in a world filled with evils, the great power of Hope has remained to try and heal the wounds.

Defeating death

■ **Christian stories say** that Jesus could raise people from the dead. He brought Lazarus back to life, even though he had been dead for four days.

■ **In Norse myth** when the god of light, Baldur, was killed, the goddess of death, Hela, said she would give him back his life if every living thing in the universe wept for him. All things wept except one – the evil god Loki.

■ **The Khoi people** of South Africa tell a tale in which a man called Tsui'goab defeated death in a wrestling match to save his village from perishing in a drought.

■ **Greek hero Heracles once wrestled** death to win back the life of a woman called Alcestis, the wife of his friend King Admetus.

■ **The Hindu lord of death, Yama**, had a child by a human woman, but did not tell her who he really was. When the child, Yama-Kumar, grew up, he blackmailed his father into keeping a sick princess alive, by threatening to tell his mother that he was actually the lord of death.

■ **In Russian myth**, Koschchei is a wizard who cheats death by keeping his soul hidden inside an egg, inside a duck, inside a hare, inside an iron chest, under an oak tree, on an island in the middle of a wide ocean.

■ **According to Greek myth**, an elderly couple called Philemon and Baucis were such good people that the gods granted them a wish – to die at the same time. The gods turned them into trees. The branches of the trees twined around each other in an eternal embrace.

■ **Inanna, the Sumerian goddess of love and war** was sentenced to death by the goddess of the dead, Ereshkigal. Inanna managed to save her own life by forfeiting the life of her husband, Damuzi.

■ **In a jealous rage**, the Hawaiian volcano goddess, Pele, once tried to kill her sister, Hi'iaka, and her love, Lohiau. Hi'iaka survived and united Lohiau's spirit with his body, bringing him back to life.

■ **In Greek mythology**, the sinner Sisyphus tried to cheat Thanatos, or death, by chaining him up. Ares, the god of war, set death free and Sisyphus was punished for eternity in the underworld.

◄ *King Arthur's knights were once challenged by a giant Green Knight to cut off his head. Sir Gawain bravely volunteered. However, the Green Knight just picked up his head and stuck it back on again!*

The Death of Baldur

A Norse myth

Baldur and his twin brother, Hodur, were the sons of the chief god, Odin and the beautiful Queen Frigg. Although they loved their sons dearly, Baldur was their clear favourite. Hodur had been born blind, and so could not share the joys of life in the same way as his brother. Yet, the twins loved one another very much. Baldur was often found with his arm linked through Hodur's, making sure he wasn't left out and lonely.

Baldur not only lifted the heart of Hodur, but of everyone in Asgard. Every god and goddess always cheered up at the sight of Baldur's shining face.

Baldur was also loved by all the humans of Midgard. Over time, Baldur became deeply troubled by nightmares of death. He could no longer smile. Instead, the light went from his eyes and his forehead became creased with a permanent furrow.

For the humans of Midgard, there was no greater joy than to die a courageous death on the battlefield. The daughters of the great god Odin himself, Valkyries, would then swoop down and take them away to live in Valhalla, the hall of the slain. There they would feast and fight to their heart's content for ever more. However, humans dreaded wasting away of old age or sickness, for then their spirits would drift down into the silent underground kingdom of Niflheim, ruled by the ghoulish queen, Hel. Baldur became consumed by a feeling of impending doom. His nightmares vividly showed his descent into the underworld for eternity, though he knew not how or why.

When Odin saw how tormented his beloved son had become, he disguised himself as a messenger, mounted his eight-legged horse Sleipnir, and raced out of Asgard faster than lightning. Without stopping, he rode furiously until finally he crossed the bridge over the black stream that bordered Hel's kingdom. Odin searched the land of the dead until he found the grey barrow of the prophetess, Volva the Wise. Chanting the strongest words of ancient magic, Odin watched as the dead woman rose, pale and ghastly, from the earth. "Tell me, who shall cause the death of my son, Baldur the Bright?" the father of the gods demanded.

"Hodur shall take his life," Volva the Wise whispered, sinking back into her grave with a great sigh.

Odin felt as though his heart was breaking as he rode the long pathways back to Asgard. Desperately, he tried to devise a way to cheat destiny, to save each of his sons from their terrible fates.

As Odin entered the halls of his palace, Queen Frigg threw her arms around him. "Put aside your fears!" she laughed. "I have saved our son! I have journeyed around the universe and spoken with every bird, every insect and every animal; every leaf, every twig, and every blossom; every dwarf, every troll, and every giant; every illness, every disease, and every poison; every man, every woman, and every child. All things under the heavens have sworn an oath not to hurt our beloved Baldur!"

"Can this really be true?" breathed Odin, a spark of hope flickering inside him.

"Come and see for yourself," Queen Frigg laughed. She led her husband away to the lush garden of Gladsheim, where a crowd of gods and goddesses had gathered, cheering and clapping with glee. Making his way to the front of the throng, he saw for himself what was entertaining them so delightfully. A chill ran down Odin's spine. The gods and goddesses were taking turns to throw objects at Baldur. They were lobbing rocks, firing arrows and hurling knives. However, to Odin's astonishment, the missiles were turning themselves and veering aside from his son, who was beaming and laughing once more. Odin could hardly believe his eyes, but at the same time he was deeply comforted. Heaving a sigh of relief, he allowed himself to smile.

Amid all the laughter, Loki, the troublemaker god, stepped forward. "Shame on you all!" he cried, bringing the sport to a halt. "You are all forgetting poor Hodur! Is no one going to help him join in the fun? Come on, Hodur. Your old friend Loki will take care of you. You want to have a go, don't you?"

Everyone began cheering once more. "Yes, Hodur – have a go!" they cried. "Come and take your turn. No matter what you do, your brother will come to no harm."

Hodur was embarrassed and protested, but Loki insisted,

giving him a dart of mistletoe. Then Loki guided Hodur's hand in the right direction, and urged, "One … two … three … fire!" The mistletoe dart sped from his fingers.

Hodur realized at once that something was terribly wrong. The crowd around him suddenly fell silent – then terrible screams and wailing tore through the air. The mistletoe dart had fired straight into Baldur's chest and pierced his heart! The stunned god had fallen to the ground and now lay dying.

"NO!" bellowed Odin. "How can this be!" With a roar, he drew his sword to smite Loki – but the sly god had vanished silently.

"It is my fault. Mine!" howled Queen Frigg, on her knees in the dirt, cradling her son's lifeless body. "I never dreamed that a tiny shoot of mistletoe might somehow be of harm. The plant was the one thing in the universe I forgot to make take an oath."

Although the tragedy was no accident, it was certainly not the fault of Queen Frigg. The jealous, cunning Loki had somehow found out her mistake and engineered Baldur's murder. With his pale body in his mother's arms, Baldur's spirit rose up and drifted away towards the murky gloom of the underworld. In his grief, Odin swore that he would track the trickster down to the ends of the earth, and make Loki regret his evil deed for all eternity.

Spirit journeys

■ **Many ancient tribal peoples** believed that their holy leaders, or shamans, could leave their bodies and journey through the spirit world.

■ **Polynesian myth tells that the dead** walk down a path called Mahiki, through a seaside cave, to reach the world of spirits, Lua-o-Milu.

■ **Mayan belief states** that the road to the underworld was steep and dangerous. It was covered with thorns, and gushing torrents of water tried to sweep souls away into abysses on either side.

■ **A story from the Book of Genesis** in the Bible tells that Jacob once saw angels going up and down a ladder between earth and heaven.

◄ *Shamans often wear costumes or masks to help them pass easily into the spirit world. This shaman in ritual dress is from the Asmat region of Africa.*

▶ *The Hopi people of North America created kachina, or spirit figures, to honour the spirits of the sun, winds, rain and maize plants (their traditional staple food).*

■ **According to classical myth**, Charon was the ferryman who sailed souls to the underworld.

■ **Native Americans believed** that souls had to cross a bridge to the afterlife guarded by the Owl Woman. She threw unidentified souls into an abyss below.

■ **In Muslim stories**, Al Sirat is the bridge to heaven. It is narrower than a spider's thread and sharper than a sword. Wicked souls fall off it and tumble down to hell.

■ **Ancient Persian stories** say that the Chinvat bridge to heaven is guarded by an angel called Rashnu. He holds golden scales to weigh the souls of the dead.

■ **In ancient Egypt** souls travelled to the underworld by boat, steered by a ferryman called Aken.

■ **Hindus cremate bodies** of the dead on the sacred river Ganges. Then the dead person's soul would be freed from its body and continue its spiritual journey.

Egyptian afterlife

■ **The ancient Egyptians** believed that people could enjoy life after death by preserving the body through mummification, putting food and personal possessions in their tomb and following elaborate funeral rites.

■ **Part of the mummification process** involved removing the internal organs and storing them in canopic jars.

■ **Each mummy** had a mask, so the spirit could recognize its body in the afterlife.

■ **It was thought** that people would work in the afterlife, so models of their tools were buried with them. Pharaohs were buried with model servants called ushabtis.

■ **Funeral rites originated** from the funeral that the god Horus gave to his father, Osiris. These were written in The Book of the Dead.

■ **One important funeral rite** was called the Opening of the Mouth ceremony. They believed it enabled the deceased to speak in the afterlife.

■ **Egyptian myth** says that the dead person's soul, or ka, was brought to an underworld Hall of Judgement.

■ **First, the jackal-headed god**, Anubis, weighed their heart against the feather of truth and justice, belonging to the goddess, Maat. If the heart was heavier than the feather, it was devoured by the crocodile-headed god, Ammut.

■ **If the heart was lighter than the feather**, the god Horus led the soul to be welcomed into the underworld by the king of the dead, Osiris.

■ **Historians believe that ancient Egyptians** built pyramid tombs to please the gods and better their chances for life after death.

▼ *Mummification was skilled work and took many weeks to complete. Firstly, the organs were removed, except the heart. Then the body was covered in salt and left to dry for about 40 days. After being washed, the dried body was stuffed so it would keep its shape. Finally, it was oiled and wrapped in layers of linen bandages.*

Osiris, King of the Dead

An ancient Egyptian myth

T he great goddess Isis was deep in mourning for her beloved husband, the god Osiris, king of Egypt. Isis knew that Osiris had been murdered by his wicked brother Seth, but she did not know how. Neither did Isis know where Osiris' body lay. However, she was determined to find out.

Disguising herself as an ordinary Egyptian, Isis spent days among the people, asking if they had seen or heard anything unusual. She wandered all over the land, but found nothing. In great despair, she entered the final village on her journey and came across a group of children. Excitedly, they told Isis that the river Nile had recently flooded, breaking its banks, and they had seen an amazing golden chest caught in the current of the churning, swirling waters. Isis' heart leapt. Perhaps this had something to do with her husband's death?

Isis hurried along the course of the Nile, searching for the golden chest. She followed the mighty river to the ocean, then continued around the coastline. Eventually, she reached the kingdom of Byblos, but there was still no sign on the golden chest. Again, Isis began asking questions, searching for any clues. Although the people knew nothing of a chest, they told her about

a huge, strong tree that had suddenly grown on the shore. The king of Byblos had admired its magnificence so much that it had been chopped down and taken to his palace. The royal craftsmen had set to work, intricately carving and painting the tree, until they had transformed it into a magnificent pillar. The pillar now stood in the throne room of the palace.

Hoping that the strange tree must have something to do with the golden chest and her husband, Isis fled to the palace at once. Every entrance was surrounded by guards and ferocious dogs roamed the grounds, leaving a frustrated Isis hiding in the bushes until nightfall. As the palace fell silent, she slipped inside through an open window. Eventually, she came across the throne room where the new pillar stood gleaming in the moonlight. With her heart pounding, she reached out and touched the smooth, richly coloured wood. Magic leapt through her fingers and flooded her veins, leaving her in a trance. Straight away, she saw a vision of what had happened to her beloved Osiris.

In spite, Seth had tricked Osiris, locked him inside the golden chest and thrown into the Nile. Unable to escape, Osiris had suffocated. After some time, the chest had eventually become dislodged from the muddy riverbed and had ended up at Byblos. There, entangled in the roots of a young tree, magic from the dead god inside the chest had made the tree grow strong and tall. With a surge of joy, Isis realized that the chest had been brought to the palace – inside the pillar! She had found her husband's body at last!

Isis decided to reveal her true nature to the king and queen of Byblos and begged the rulers to allow her to cut Osiris' golden coffin out of the pillar. Of course, the king and queen agreed and the very next day, the goddess sailed home with her precious cargo. During the voyage, Isis thought hard about where she could hide Osiris' coffin, so that his body would be safe forever. Upon reaching Egypt, Isis headed for a remote swamp, where she hid

Osiris' coffin in the boggy waters. She was sure no one would ever find it there …

Unfortunately, the evil Seth had spies everywhere. Isis had barely arrived back at her palace before Seth had his hands on the golden chest once more. Although furious that his brother's dead body had come back to haunt him, Seth was also rightly wary of Isis' immense knowledge and magic powers. He feared that Isis might know the secret of life itself, and be able to bring Osiris back from the dead! In desperation, the black-hearted ruler drew his sword, chopping Osiris' body into fourteen pieces. Then using his magic, he scattered them far and wide across Egypt.

When Isis discovered that the golden coffin was gone from the swamp and her dead husband's body was missing again, her weeping and wailing reached the far ends of the country. The goddess Nephthys tried to comfort her, offering her help in the search for Osiris.

It was a long, long time before Isis and Nephthys found the first part of Osiris' body – his head. Horrified by Seth's treachery, the goddesses continued their search. After countless days and nights, they found every piece of Osiris' body and took them to the jackal-headed god Anubis, guardian of graveyards. Anubis not only had the power to restore the great god's body, but he could also preserve it for eternity.

Anubis carefully removed all the organs and put them into canopic jars for storage. Then he washed Osiris' body with wine and covered it with salts. After forty days, Osiris' skin was dried and preserved, and ready to be cleaned. Finally, Anubis filled the stomach with the fragrant spices of frankincense and myrrh, wrapped the body in bandages and placed it in a coffin, guarded by spells. The wise god Thoth had used powerful magic to put a terrible curse on anyone who touched it. Anubis promised to stand guard over it, day and night. Isis knelt and wept. But this time her tears were of relief, rather than sorrow.

Unbeknown to Isis, at the time Osiris was murdered, she was in fact pregnant with his child. She was overjoyed when she gave birth to their son, Horus, who grew up into one of the bravest and strongest of the gods. When Horus came of age, he challenged his wicked uncle Seth, and won back the throne of Egypt. King Horus' first command was that his father's body should finally be given a proper burial.

An enormous tomb was built and Osiris' mummy carried there in a magnificent procession. Horus said prayers for his father, then the mummy was sealed inside the tomb. At long last, Osiris' spirit was released from its dead body, destined for the underworld. In a grand ceremony, Osiris was appointed king of the dead by the great creator, Ra, and he now stands in judgement over the spirits of the deceased.

As a reward for her devotion, Isis is able to descend to the underworld to see her beloved husband, and then return safely to earth to live with her precious son, Horus.

Entering the realm of the dead

■ **In Greek mythology**, a poet called Orpheus once ventured down to the underworld to try to bring back his dead wife, Eurydice. He was only allowed to take her back to the land of the living if on the journey from the underworld, he refrained from looking at her.

■ **According to Chinese myth**, a Buddhist monk once entered the underworld to search for the soul of his mother. The gods ended up keeping him there as the ruler.

■ **Greek myth says** that when the god of the dead, Hades, kidnapped Persephone, the messenger god, Hermes, went into the underworld to persuade Hades to let her go.

■ **In Norse myth**, the messenger god Hermod volunteered to go to the underworld to try to bring the god Baldur back to life.

■ **The Harrowing of Hell** is a legend that says Jesus journeyed into hell and triumphed over evils there in the three days between his death and resurrection.

■ **In the Roman epic** *Aeneid*, the hero Aeneas travels to the underworld. The ghost of his father shows him a line of souls that are waiting to be born as his descendants.

■ **The Mayan creator god**, Hunahpu, travelled into the underworld with his brother, Ixbalangue. There they killed two demons, Hun Came and Vucub Caquix.

■ **The Greek hero Odysseus** went into the underworld to ask a dead seer, Tiresias, how he could find his way home from the Trojan Wars.

■ **The ancient Egyptian** sun god, Ra, sailed through the underworld every night to fight demons and other evils.

■ **A Thracian people believed** that the god Zalmoxis lived among humans. He once disappeared into the underworld for three years to teach people about the immortality of the soul.

▼ *The falcon-headed Egyptian sun god sailed at night through the underworld. The light of Ra was so powerful that he was able to resurrect the dead.*

Persephone and the Pomegranate Seed

An ancient Greek myth

*O*f all the gods and goddesses on Mount Olympus, Demeter loved the earth and its mortals the most. The great goddess of the harvest, she taught people how to plant, raise and reap grain, fruits and vegetables. In return, mortals loved Demeter dearly. Each mealtime, farmers' wives would set an extra place at the table, hoping that the goddess would grace them with her presence.

Demeter and the mighty father of the gods, Zeus, had a daughter, Persephone, who was their greatest joy. A beautiful girl, she cherished the earth, just like her mother. Persephone delighted in roaming the world, picking wild flowers in sunny meadows, and appreciating the splendour and beauty all around her.

One day, the goddess of love and beauty, Aphrodite, looked down from Mount Olympus. She smiled, catching sight of Persephone and her two best friends, the goddesses Athene and Artemis, enjoying themselves. Out of the corner of her eye, she also noticed the ruler of the underworld, Hades, riding through the sky in his black chariot.

Hades often left his dark kingdom to survey the earth above. The Titans, who had been imprisoned deep inside the world, were forever writhing about, trying to shake off their chains, and breathing fire in their fury. Hades had to watch that the earthquakes and volcanoes they caused were not tearing asunder the roof of his kingdom.

A sudden idea came to Aphrodite. She smiled mischeviously. None of the three goddesses, nor Hades, had ever been in love. But she could change all that. She quickly worked some magic, then sat back to watch the fun …

Sure enough, it wasn't long before Hades marched into Zeus' throne room. "Brother," the king of the underworld announced, "I am in torment. I have fallen deeply in love with your daughter, Persephone, and cannot rest for longing. I have come to ask for her hand in marriage. I swear that I will love her for eternity and do everything in my power to make her happy."

Zeus was pleased. The mighty king of a vast kingdom, Hades was a wise and fair ruler. He owned all the wealth of the earth, including diamonds and emeralds.

"I can think of no one better as a husband for Persephone," Zeus assured his brother. "However, I fear that Demeter will not allow it. She will never see her daughter taken from the sunshine that she loves to live underground – no matter how excellent a husband you are."

Hades groaned. "Brother, believe me, I know this too well –
and I have tried my hardest to forget Persephone. My thoughts are
filled with her, day and night. I can admire no other. If I cannot
have Persephone as my wife, I fear my heart will break and I will
never recover from such sorrow."

Zeus thought for a moment. "If asking Demeter will bring
certain rejection, do not ask her. Seize Persephone and sweep her
away. By the time Demeter finds out, it will be too late for her to

do anything." Hades embraced his brother, then strode away, determinedly.

The very next day, Persephone, Athene and Artemis were laughing and playing in the woods, when in a clearing, Persephone spotted a flower she had never seen before. Delighted at its shimmering colours and delicate petals, she stooped to breathe in its sweet fragrance.

Suddenly, a thunderous rumble shook the earth and the ground opened wide. Out of underworld came a gleaming, black chariot pulled by two wild-eyed horses. Persephone tried to run but she was quickly seized by a strong arm and swept up into the arms of the dark lord himself. Hades had come to collect his love. Galloping faster than the wind, the horses sprang away across the earth.

Athene and Artemis fell to their knees in the quake, and didn't see Hades take Persephone. On hearing her scream, they span round to find that she had vanished. The bunch of flowers she had been picking were strewn around a gaping fissure in the earth. The panicked goddesses ran back and forth, desperately calling her name – but the only reply was the agitated bowing of the plants in the breeze and the alarmed rustling of the leaves.

Meanwhile, Persephone was held tightly in Hades' grasp as the chariot sped across fields and forests, mountains and valleys. Beside herself with terror, Persephone cried out, "Mother! Father!

Help me! Someone, please help me!" But the lord of the dead simply cracked his whip, and they galloped through the sky, far away from the gods and goddesses of Mount Olympus. Persephone's voice simply faded and died on the wind.

Fortunately, the lord of the sun Helios was journeying in his own chariot high in the sky. For one brief moment, Helios saw the frothing, straining horses, the grim-faced lord of darkness, and the horrified, screaming girl. Suddenly, the ground split in two, the horses and the chariot plunged down into the depths, and the earth sealed over them. Persephone was gone.

When Athene and Artemis told Demeter that Persephone had disappeared, the great goddess was beside herself with grief. Demeter set off across the whole world, desperately looking everywhere for her beloved child – but no one could tell her anything.

Demeter's sorrow soon turned to frustration and rage, and her anger turned on the earth and all the mortals it fed. The goddess commanded every seed to shrivel, every plant to droop, and every tree to wither. She ordered cold winds to blow, drying the soil. Then she told heavy rains to fall, washing away the earth's goodness. She prevented animals from giving birth to young. She ordered bushes not to bear fruit and vegetables not to sprout. She commanded leaves to fall from trees, covering the earth in a multi-coloured blanket.

Helios saw what was happening
from his fiery chariot, high in the heavens.
Deeply concerned, he hurried to Demeter at
once to explain what he had seen. Demeter was
not reassured or relieved at the news, and took
out her fury on the entire world. Boiling with
rage, she was determined to make all mortals suffer
as she was suffering. She would leave them to die of
starvation. Then the gods would be sorry.

Zeus was indeed deeply alarmed as he beheld his
dying world. He had underestimated Demeter's grief
and wrath and immediately sent his messenger, Hermes, to
the underworld. "Find Persephone and bring her back to
her mother," Zeus ordered Hermes. "But hurry, for if
she has eaten any of the food of the dead, she must
remain in the underworld forever!"

Hermes sped deep below the ground into the
kingdom of darkness. Kneeling before the
thrones of Hades and his new queen, he
explained that Demeter would destroy all
creation if Persephone were not
returned to the light at once. The
sorrowful girl's heart was filled with
hope at the messenger's words –

until Hermes looked sternly at her and said, "Tell me, Persephone, that you have not yet eaten the food of the dead."

Persephone's heart began to flutter. "I have," she gasped, "but only one pomegranate seed – that's all."

The king of the underworld took Persephone's hand. "You now belong to me and my kingdom, but I will not force you to stay here forever," he said gently. "You must keep me company here for only half of every year. Now, go to your mother. But remember I love you dearly. I will be counting every second until you return."

Soon Persephone and Demeter were joyfully reunited. Touched by Hades' kindness, Persephone found herself thinking fondly of the sad king sitting alone in the underworld without her. She would be glad to return to him when the time came.

Every spring and summer, Demeter rejoices that Persephone is with her and the earth flourishes. But every autumn and winter, Demeter mourns her daughter's descent into the underworld, and the earth becomes barren once more.

Visions of the end

- **Stories about the end of the world** are said to be eschatological myths. Tales about the creation of the world are called cosmogonical.

- **In the Bible**, Saint John predicts that four horsemen representing war, famine, plague and death will appear at the end of the world.

- **The Fon tribe of Africa** believe that the world is circled by a huge sea snake. One day, he will no longer be able to support the earth's weight and it will sink to the bottom of the ocean.

- **An Inca story says** that if mankind becomes too wicked, the god Viraccocha will weep a flood of tears that will sweep humans away.

- **At the end of the world**, Aztec myth states that the god Quetzalcóatl will return to the people. When the Spaniards invaded in 1519, the Aztecs believed that the Spanish leader was the returning Quetzalcóatl and so allowed themselves to be conquered.

- **In Norse myth**, Ragnarok means 'the doom of the gods'. A huge battle will take place between the forces of evil and the forces of good. Evil will win and a new universe will be born.

- **Jewish mythology** tells of an angel called Israfel. He spends all eternity holding a trumpet to his lips, ready to announce the end of the world.

- **According to Persian myth**, the end of time will begin when an imprisoned dragon, Azhi Dahaka, breaks free.

- **Islamic myth says** every person has an angel who follows them all their lives and writes down everything they do – good and bad. At the end of the world, everyone will be judged by their book of deeds.

■ **Many 20th-century people** used to think that the world would be destroyed by nuclear war. Now it is deemed more likely that a deadly virus or natural disaster will cause the end of the world.

▼ *Scientists believe that the universe may end in the Big Crunch – the opposite to the Big Bang – the universe will implode, shrinking back into nothingness.*

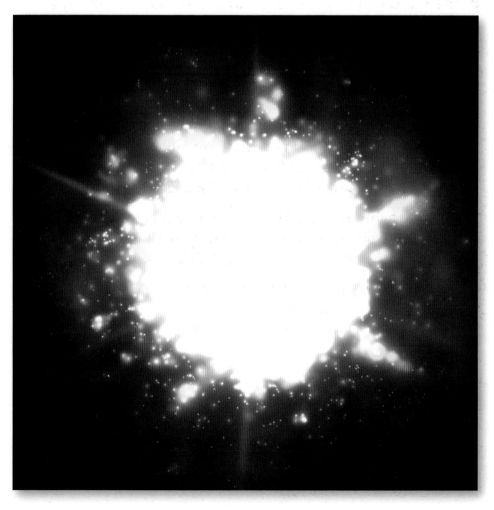

Index

Index of stories